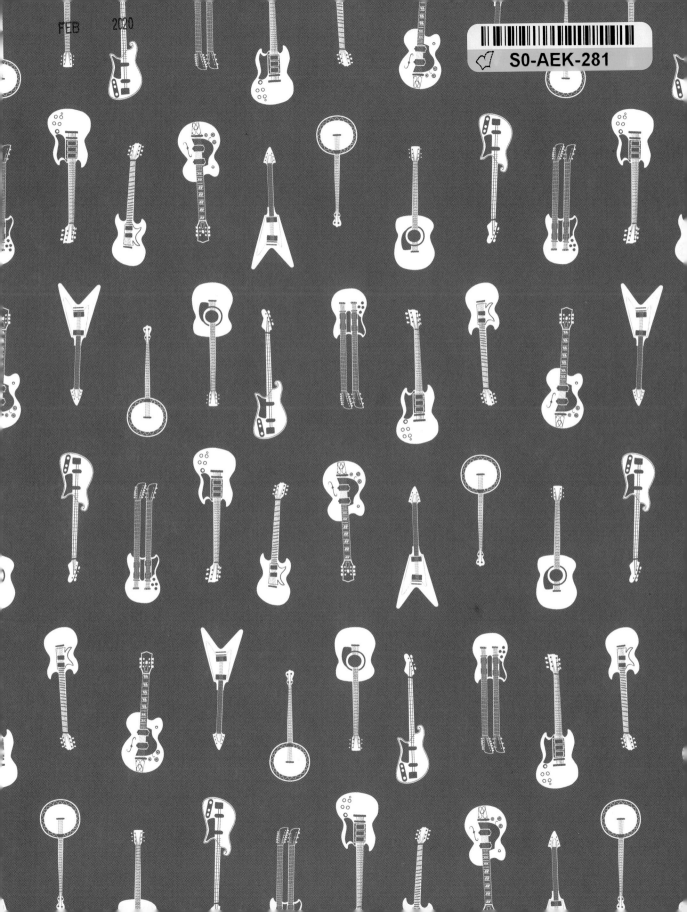

FEB 2020

THE HISTORY OF
ROCK
FOR BIG FANS AND
LITTLE PUNKS

TEXT AND RESEARCH Rita Nabais | ILLUSTRATION Joana Raimundo

30 YEARS®
TRIUMPH
BOOKS

Library of Congress Cataloging-in-Publication Data available upon request.

This book is available in quantity at special discounts for your group or organization. For further information, contact:
Triumph Books LLC
814 North Franklin Street
Chicago, Illinois 60610
(312) 337-0747
www.triumphbooks.com

Printed in U.S.A.
ISBN: 978-1-62937-733-9

Interior design: Escafandro, Associação Cultural
Cover design: Joana Raimundo
Layout: Andreia Silvano
Project editor: Nuno Matos Valente
Translation: Pedro Homero
Proofreading: Charlotte Heslop

FOR LITTLE PUNKS

For the little punks in my life: Francisco, João, Guilherme, Matilde, Maria, Vasco, Alice, Tiago, Zé Pedro, Inês, Sofia, Gonçalo and those to come.

—Rita

To all those with whom I've shared tapes, CDs and endless conversations about music. To all those with whom I've had the pleasure of attending concerts. To all those with whom I've played "band." To all those with whom I've played in make-believe bands. To my best friends.

—Joana

Inside this book you'll find the main bands and musicians in the history of *Rock* through illustrations, short overviews of their lives, special traits and trivia about each band or solo artist.

Who are the most important artists? How did they start their bands and careers? What is a *Rock* star made of?

This history of *Rock* is divided into several chapters. At the beginning of each, you'll find a short text that will explain which artists or bands you'll get to know and the reason they appear together. Apart from the illustrations, text and trivia about the musicians, you'll also find explanatory tables to learn their names, where they were born and what music genre(s) they played. There's also a section with suggestions of songs from important artists that have not been featured.

You'll understand that there are musicians from all walks of life: while some have studied music in school, others did it by themselves or with friends, and there are even those who never stopped learning and trying new things.

If you have any doubt about words you don't know, you can check the glossary at the end of the book, or the index of music genres, where you'll find more than 40 definitions. You'll find what *Rockabilly*, *Reggae*, *Punk*, *Industrial*, *Glam*, *New Wave*, *Progressive*, *Heavy Metal*, *Goth*, *Grunge* and many other words mean.

I suggest that, while reading the book, you listen to some of the recommended songs – the best way to know music is to listen to it. If you do so, and if you read the entire book, you'll become a true specialist!

FOR BIG FANS

Three essential factors aligned in order for this book to come to life: my passion for music, the fact that I'm a teacher who interacts daily with children and, finally, the realization that there are almost no books about *Rock* for children. This was the determining factor in embarking on this music epic targeted at children but winking at adults too.

There are many ways to write about the history of music, particularly *Rock*. Each writer approaches the subject in a different way – their own way of listening to and understanding music. In this book I tried to follow the history's timeline, highlighting the most important artists and bands. I measured an artist's relevance by the level of influence they had on others and by the depth of their mark on our culture. This required investigative work consisting of research, as well as structuring, listening to and categorizing hundreds of bands. In order to avoid making it too personal, I perused books and reference websites, different top charts from magazines and field experts, lists of essential bands curated by musicians and music lovers (whom I thank elsewhere in this book) and also websites and biographies from the bands them-

selves. Still, I've surely left out some artists that should have been highlighted, but space is finite.

I was fortunate enough to work with a talented team: Nuno, my project editor, who had the demanding work of trimming unnecessary fat and improving many of the texts; Joana, who has materialized my ideas for each artist or band in art form; Andreia, who brought all the parts together without ever failing a deadline. This team was joined by Pedro, the translator, who turned out to be much more than that; being passionate about music, he didn't leave a loose end. Finally, Charlotte came aboard and reviewed the English text to make it bulletproof.

I made an effort to keep in mind that this book, which may be of interest to adults, was conceived of and written for children. Therefore, I tried to find funny anecdotes in the artists' history and softened the language in order to make it fun to read the book.

I've wondered many times if the reason for this project's existence lies actually in my own childhood, in the pleasure that I would have drawn from reading such a book, one that would reveal to me a less obvious musical realm in a way I could understand.

—Rita Nabais

INDEX

In the early 1950s a musical earthquake called *Rock and Roll* shook the United States of America. The sounds and traditions coming from different places, like the African rhythms and the melodies sung by European emigrants, blended for the first time. People from all races, creeds and origins, working side by side and listening to each other singing their songs, influenced one another and fused their traditions in a rich cultural melting pot that would create the music that is simply known as *Rock*. The energy-filled rhythms and the simple and saucy language struck a chord, especially with adolescents. A lot of musicians started *Rock and Roll*'s journey, but in these pages you'll find some of those that placed *Rock* in the history of music.

The band's name, Bill Haley & His Comets, was inspired by Halley's Comet. As Bill's surname was pronounced the same way he decided to create a pun, adding his Comets to Haley.

WOP BOP A LOO BOP A LOP BAM BOOM

He was really eccentric, played like a madman, had long hair and sang a lot of uuuhhhs!

BILL HALEY & HIS COMETS

At the start of his career, Bill Haley played and sang *Country* songs and then later *R&B*. One day he decided to mix these two styles in a single song called *Crazy, Man, Crazy*. Young kids went wild with it! That was when Haley decided to change both the style of his songs and of himself; he swapped his cowboy outfit with a checkered jacket, covered his hair with pomade (which is similar to hair gel) and started styling a big curl of it on his forehead. Bill Haley & His Comets were playing and singing *Rock and Roll* even before the name was invented. Together they recorded two of the most famous songs in the history of *Rock*: *Rock Around the Clock* and *Shake, Rattle and Roll*.

DEBUT ALBUM 1953

ORIGIN Chester, PA

GENRE Rock and Roll, Country, Rockabilly

FAMOUS SONGS
Rock Around the Clock
Shake, Rattle and Roll
See You Later, Alligator

LITTLE RICHARD

Little Richard was one of the first *Rock and Roll* stars. Even as a child, growing up in a 12 child household, he loved to sing. He was 10 when he performed live for the first time and by 14 he had left his parents' house to follow travelling musical acts. His songs were based on a magical formula: fast and explosive piano playing coupled with lyrics filled with words that made no sense, sung in a high-pitched voice. His first major hit was *Tutti Frutti*, a song that starts with the sentence "Wop bop a loo bop a lop bam boom!", whatever that means.

DEBUT ALBUM 1957

ORIGIN Macon, GA

GENRE Rock and Roll, R&B, Gospel, Soul

FAMOUS SONGS
Tutti Frutti
Lucille
Long Tall Sally
Good Golly, Miss Molly

CHUCK BERRY

The intros to his songs, with the unforgettable sound of the electric guitar and catchy melodies, made him one of the *Rock and Roll* pioneers. Fans loved Chuck's concerts and the way he dressed and moved on stage. He was always very clean cut: three-piece black suit, white shirt and bow tie, with hair pulled all the way back with a lot of pomade. Before he became a musician he worked at an automobile assembly plant and as a hairdresser, which might explain why he was so stylish. One of his biggest fans was a boy named Keith Richards, who would later become the guitar player in one of the biggest *Rock* bands in the world: The Rolling Stones.

He had this strange way of criss-crossing the stage, in a duck-like fashion.

DEBUT ALBUM 1957

ORIGIN St. Louis, MO

GENRE Rock and Roll

FAMOUS SONGS
Roll Over Beethoven
Rock and Roll Music
Johnny B. Goode
You Never Can Tell

JERRY LEE LEWIS

Jerry Lee Lewis started playing the piano when he was 8. He played so well, in fact, that upon hearing it his parents decided to sell the house in order to buy him a piano (pianos are expensive instruments). He was 21 when he travelled to the city of Memphis where he would record his first songs for the best well-known label in town, *Sun Records*. To help pay for the trip they had to raise chickens and sell eggs – lots of eggs. It was there that he recorded all his initial hits: *Crazy Arms*, *Whole Lotta Shakin' Going On* and *Great Balls of Fire*. Lewis was one of the most influential *Rock and Roll* pianists in the history of music. Elvis Presley once said that if he played the piano like Jerry he wouldn't even have to sing.

DEBUT ALBUM 1958

ORIGIN Ferriday, LA

GENRE Rock and Roll, Rockabilly, Country, Gospel, Blues

FAMOUS SONGS
Great Balls of Fire
Crazy Arms
Whole Lotta Shakin' Goin' On

Jerry played the piano with almost every part of his body and he even set a piano on fire during a concert!

7

The Beatles were fans of Holly and their name drew inspiration from him.

His black rimmed glasses were his trademark.

BUDDY HOLLY

Buddy learned how to play the piano and the violin but he was a bit clumsy, so his older brothers taught him guitar basics. Upon finishing high school, he formed a *Country* band. Their songs were played on the local radio station and they became Lubbock's supporting act to bands that came to town to play. Buddy's life changed when he saw Elvis Presley in concert for the first time and later played in a concert headlined by the King of *Rock* himself: he became converted to *Rock and Roll*. By 1956 Buddy and his newly named band The Crickets started to record some songs, including one of their biggest hits, *That'll Be the Day*. Buddy wrote and played his own songs which was quite uncommon because at that time music labels hired composers and session musicians. His brilliant career was just getting started when a tragic airplane accident ended it prematurely. It inspired Don McLean's famous song *American Pie*.

DEBUT ALBUM 1957

ORIGIN Lubbock, TX

GENRE Rock and Roll, Rockabilly

FAMOUS SONGS
That'll Be the Day
Peggy Sue
Everyday

WANDA JACKSON

Wanda got her first guitar when she was 6. Having a *Country* musician as a father helped her get into music from a tender age. She attended live concerts and sang in her church choir. By 1956, at the age of 19 she won a talent show and got her own radio show as a prize. Music labels started to get interested in Wanda and soon she was playing *Country* music live with her father, wearing the fancy clothes mom made for her. She toured with Elvis and they even dated for a little while. The King encouraged her to sing *Rock and Roll* and boy did Wanda love it! Her looks were unique: short dresses, guitar in her hands and hip-shaking moves. In the '50s this was a heresy! Wanda was one of the first women to play and sing *Rock and Roll* and became known as the *Rockabilly* Queen.

In 2001 she recorded a covers album with Jack White, from The White Stripes.

DEBUT ALBUM 1958

ORIGIN Maud, OK

GENRE Rock and Roll, Gospel, Country, Rockabilly

FAMOUS SONGS
I Gotta Know
Funnel of Love
Hard-Headed Woman
Let's Have a Party

ELVIS PRESLEY

Elvis Presley fell in love with music at an early age. As soon as he finished high school, he got a job as a truck driver and saved enough money to record his first songs as a gift to his mother. The owner of the label liked his voice so much that he decided to hire him on the spot. From that moment on, Elvis's songs became instant hits, one after the other. He was 23 when he became a film actor, which increased his popularity even more. His extravagant and bold dance moves at his concerts made the audience scream wildly – especially girls. A lot of musicians had started playing and singing in the same music genre before him, but Elvis was the one who made *Rock and Roll* reach every corner of the US and the rest of the world. Elvis Presley is known worldwide as the King of *Rock* and to this day nobody has claimed his title! He remains beloved by fans, and to this day there are many who believe Elvis hasn't died.

Elvis' favorite sandwich had peanut butter, bacon, banana and honey. What a hodgepodge!

OTHER MUSICIANS
be all ears

SISTER ROSETTA THARPE
Up Above My Head
Didn't It Rain

FATS DOMINO
Blueberry Hill
Ain't That a Shame

BO DIDDLEY
I'm a Man
Bo Diddley

CARL PERKINS
Blue Suede Shoes
Matchbox

THE EVERLY BROTHERS
Wake Up Little Susie
All I Have to do is Dream

RITCHIE VALENS
Come On, Let's Go
La Bamba

DEBUT ALBUM 1956

ORIGIN Tupelo, MS

GENRE Rock and Roll, Pop, Rockabilly, Country, Blues, Gospel, R&B

FAMOUS SONGS
Jailhouse Rock
Love Me Tender
All Shook Up
Don't Be Cruel
Hound Dog

It's only fair to ask what are these *Country* musicians – coming from a traditional musical style – doing in a book on *Rock*. This type of question will pop up often, but the answer is simple: Johnny Cash, especially, was a rebel and his music was simple and direct, just like *Rock* itself. *Rock* isn't just a music style – it's also an attitude. Besides, these musicians were and still are admired by a lot of *Rock* artists.

JOHNNY CASH

Johnny's musical career started right about the time *Rock and Roll* was breaking out, yet his heart was in *Country* music. At 12 he was already writing songs inspired by this traditional style which he heard on the radio. He worked in cotton fields and at an automobile plant, and also served in the Air Force, yet despite the harshness of these jobs he taught himself how to play the guitar and got to record his first songs by 23. He achieved a lot of success, but his rebelliousness made him go astray and landed him in prison seven times. When free, he enjoyed playing in prisons because he empathized with the inmates. He had a deep, cavernous voice and a sad, humble and dark look, which gave him the nickname "Man in Black." Johnny Cash was a *Rock* fan, so much so that in the last stage of his career Cash covered several *Rock* artists. Some of them are in this book, like The Beatles, Bruce Springsteen, Nick Cave, Depeche Mode, Beck, and Nine Inch Nails, among others. Despite having been one of the greatest *Country* artists of all time, Johnny has become a reference in the history of *Rock*.

Johnny Cash knew how to hypnotize himself (if you believe that sort of stuff)!

DEBUT ALBUM 1956

ORIGIN Kingsland, AR

GENRE Rock and Roll, Country, Folk, Gospel

FAMOUS SONGS

I Walk the Line

Folsom Prison Blues

Ring of Fire

OTHER MUSICIANS
be all ears

HANK WILLIAMS
Hey, Good Lookin'
I'm So Lonesome I Could Cry

MERLE HAGGARD
Mama Tried
Okie from Muskogee

THE BAND
Up on Cripple Creek
The Night They Drove Old Dixie Down

EMMYLOU HARRIS
Two More Bottles of Wine
Tulsa Queen

KENNY ROGERS
Coward of the County
The Gambler

EAGLES
New Kid in Town
Hotel California

A little before his 81st birthday, in 2014, Willie showed his great physical shape by winning his fifth degree black belt in GongKwon Yusul, a martial art.

WILLIE NELSON

Willie and his older sister were raised by their grandparents who loved music and passed this passion to their grandchildren, teaching them how to play the guitar and piano. By 1939 his grandfather gave him his first guitar; he was only 6 years old and the following year he started writing songs. He enlisted in the Air Force, studied agriculture and worked as a Radio DJ but never forgot his passion for *Country* music. In 1960 he moved to Nashville, where he started writing music for other musicians. Some of the songs he wrote for them were more successful than the ones he sang himself. Willie returned to Texas in the '70s and never stopped writing and singing. He is one of the most successful *Country* composers and musicians. At 85 he had already released 68 records and was playing between 150 and 200 concerts per year.

DEBUT ALBUM 1962

ORIGIN Abbott, TX

GENRE Country, Blues, Jazz

FAMOUS SONGS
Crazy
On the Road Again
Pancho and Lefty
Funny How Time Slips Away

DOLLY PARTON

Dolly was born into a big family with a total of 12 siblings! Her family was poor, but that did not stop her mother – who knew how to sing and play the guitar – giving Dolly a love for music. As with many artists in this book it all started with a guitar, only in this case it was even more impressive: Dolly built her own guitar when she was seven! A year later, her uncle gave her a real one. By 10 she was already playing on radio and television shows and recorded her first song when she was 13. Her career started at 21; she wrote her own lyrics and music and sang her songs (but also wrote for others) and had hit after hit since then. She recorded almost as many records as Willie Nelson and starred in many films. She's over 70 now, but is still very active and filled with ideas for new projects.

Dolly has no children of her own, but she does have a very special goddaughter – Miley Cyrus!

DEBUT ALBUM 1958

ORIGIN Locust Ridge, TN

GENRE Country

FAMOUS SONGS
Jolene
I Will Always Love You
Here You Come Again
9 to 5
Islands in the Stream

MISSISSIPPI BLUES

Blues music appeared in the USA, in the Mississippi River Delta, by the end of the 19th century. The *Blues* rhythm has roots in African musical traditions, work songs, spirituals and folk music. *Blues* gave rise to almost all the 20th century American music genres including *Jazz*, *R&B*, *Rock and Roll* and *Soul*. *Blues* gave birth to *Rock* but was also influenced by its "child": *Blues Rock* combines elements of *Blues* and *Rock and Roll* and is heavily based on the electric guitar. It started in the mid-1960s, both in England and in the United States, with bands like Cream, The Rolling Stones and Creedence Clearwater Revival, which were *Rock* bands that experimented with *Blues* songs.

Howlin' Wolf's grandfather told him scary stories about howling wolves and how they would catch him should he misbehave.

One of King's trademarks was naming his guitars "Lucille."

HOWLIN' WOLF

Chester Arthur Burnett was Howlin' Wolf's real name. Chester grew up on a cotton plantation where he heard traditional Mississippi songs. He started singing and playing the guitar at an early age; as a teenager, he was already playing some small clubs. He was influenced by some of the early *Blues* musicians: "Blind Lemon" Jefferson, "Sonny Boy" Williamson and Charley Patton. By 1948 he had formed his first band, and three years later he recorded his first song, which became a hit. By then he had moved to Chicago, where he helped transform the acoustic sound of *Blues* into an electric one. Howlin' Wolf was a great guitar and harmonica player, but his best instrument was his voice, deep and profound and filled with power and authenticity.

DEBUT ALBUM 1951

ORIGIN White Station, MS

GENRE Blues

FAMOUS SONGS
Smokestack Lightnin'
Back Door Man
Killing Floor
Spoonful

B.B. KING

Just like Howlin' Wolf, Riley Ben King was born on a Mississippi cotton plantation where his parents worked. He had a rough childhood and was raised by his maternal grandmother. At that time he sang *Gospel* in a church choir and by 12 he got his first guitar, with which he learned how to play. By the mid-1940s he moved to Memphis and became a DJ at a local radio station where he was nicknamed B.B. (for "Blues Boy"). It was on the radio that his music became successful, earning him a record contract. Throughout the next decade B.B. King stood tall as one of the biggest names in *Blues* and still reigns supreme. B.B. recorded dozens of albums and performed hundreds of concerts, giving *Blues* a new style and popularizing the genre all around the world.

DEBUT ALBUM 1956

ORIGIN Itta Bena, MS

GENRE Blues, R&B, Rock

FAMOUS SONGS
Rock Me Baby
The Thrill Is Gone

MUDDY WATERS

Like these other *Blues* artists, McKinley Morganfield grew up on a cotton plantation in the Mississippi Delta. He was raised by his grandmother and earned the nickname "Muddy" because he enjoyed playing in mud puddles. "Waters" was added to his name a few years later. By 13 he was already playing the harmonica at local parties and by 17 he had bought his first guitar, inspired by the *Delta Blues* artists. When he turned 30 he moved to Chicago, working by day as a truck driver and in a paper mill, while trying his luck as a musician by night. A few years later he recorded his first songs, and the following decade he released some of his biggest successes,

I'M A MAAAAAAN!

Keith Richards, The Rolling Stones' guitar player, stated that his band was named like that because of the Muddy Waters song with the same name. Supposedly, he had the idea when, during an interview, he saw a record on the floor, with the name of the song facing up.

DEBUT ALBUM 1960

ORIGIN Issaquena County, MS

GENRE Blues

FAMOUS SONGS
Mannish Boy
Hoochie Coochie Man
I Just Want to Make Love to You

becoming one of the most influential musicians in the genre.

Despite being fast with the guitar, Eric Clapton was nicknamed "Slowhand".

ERIC CLAPTON

Unlike the others in this chapter, Eric Clapton was born in England. He's a lot younger, too! He got a guitar for his 13th birthday. He wasn't able to play it immediately, so he gave up, but after a while he picked it up again and never stopped again. He played old *Blues* records on a loop until he was able to play them by heart. He was playing so well that he dropped out of art school. By 17, he started his first band and joined The Yardbirds in 1963, leaving right about the time the band got some success. He went through a couple of projects before joining Cream, who (despite having lasted only two years) are considered one of the most important bands of their time. By then, Eric was already considered one of the best guitar players in England. After being part of so many bands he ended up becoming a solo artist, achieving enormous success. He is still considered one of the all-time best guitarists in the world.

DEBUT ALBUM 1970
Yardbirds (1964)
Cream (1966)

ORIGIN Ripley

GENRE Blues, Rock

FAMOUS SONGS
Tears in Heaven
Layla
Wonderful Tonight

OTHER MUSICIANS
be all ears

JOHN LEE HOOKER
Crawling King Snake
Boom Boom

LYNYRD SKYNYRD
Free Bird
Sweet Home Alabama

THE JEFF BECK GROUP
Going Down
Situation

SANTANA
Black Magic Woman
Oye Como Va

STEVIE RAY VAUGHAN
Look at Little Sister
Little Wing

THE ALLMAN BROTHERS BAND
Midnight Rider
Ramblin' Man

DR. FEELGOOD
She Does It Right
Roxette

DIRE STRAITS
Sultans of Swing
Brothers in Arms

Throughout this book you will find several artists who had really important music careers and influenced a lot of *Rock* musicians (as well as being influenced by them), despite not being rockers themselves. You see, music genres are more of an art form than a science, and it's not possible to draw rigid borders between them. These musicians' unique voices, writing, singing, and even dancing styles had an impact on many artists that appeared in the following decades and who drew inspiration from *Soul* and *R&B* to write their songs, doing what *Rock* does best: mixing and matching, influencing and being influenced.

Ray Charles became blind at 7.

RAY CHARLES

At 7, when Ray lost his sight, his mother sent him to a special school (for the deaf and the blind) where he learned to read Braille and to play the piano, the clarinet and the saxophone. Ray's loss of sight made him develop a skilled memory for music as well as "absolute pitch" which is the ability to identify the musical note of any sound you hear. By 1955, *Rock and Roll* broke out: Elvis was a hit and black singers like Chuck Berry and Little Richard became *Rock* stars. Ray took the opportunity to release hits like *I Got a Woman*, *What I'd Say*, and *Hit the Road Jack*, among many others, fusing elements from *R&B*, *Jazz*, *Blues*, *Country* and *Gospel* in his songs. You could say that this mix of genres paved the way for '60s *Soul*, making him a beloved star to artists from several different music genres. Ray Charles became known as "The Father of *Soul*."

DEBUT ALBUM 1954

ORIGIN Albany, GA

GENRE R&B, Soul, Blues, Gospel, Jazz, Country, Pop, Rock and Roll

FAMOUS SONGS

What'd I Say

I Got a Woman

Hit the Road Jack (popularized by)

Georgia On My Mind

Sam Cooke's music was appreciated both by young people and their parents.

SAM COOKE

For many, Sam Cooke is the inventor of the *Soul* genre. As a teenager, he sang in a *Gospel* choir, but a few years after that he decided to leave *Gospel* and create his own style. He had a most beautiful and magical voice, which makes those who listen to it want to sing like him. Thanks to the natural beauty of his voice he went down in history as one of the best singers ever. You may not know his name but one of his songs is so pretty and popular that it is heard in many settings globally: *Wonderful World*.

DEBUT ALBUM 1957

ORIGIN Clarksdale, MS

GENRE Soul, Gospel, R&B

FAMOUS SONGS

Wonderful World

You Send Me

A Change Is Gonna Come

Cupid

ARETHA FRANKLIN

Aretha was a natural born singer and pianist, sort of a child prodigy. She used to sing in the church where her father was minister. She interpreted *Gospel* with such intensity that by 14 she was recording some songs in that musical genre. In the first half of the 1960s, she recorded 10 albums, but the label (Columbia Records) wasn't truly able to bring out her vocal talent and *Soul*. When she switched labels her hits converted into gold records (which means that 500,000 copies of each record were sold) and then later platinum (1,000,000 copies sold). Songs like *Respect* or *I Say a Little Prayer* gave Aretha the title of Queen of *Soul*. She was considered the greatest singer of all time not just for her vocal skills but also for the depth that she poured into her songs.

In 1987 Aretha was the first woman to be inducted in the Rock and Roll Hall of Fame.

R-E-S-P-E-C-T

DEBUT ALBUM 1961

ORIGIN Memphis, TN

GENRE Soul, R&B, Gospel

FAMOUS SONGS

Chain Of Fools

Respect

I Say a Little Prayer

(You Make Me Feel Like) A Natural Woman

Think

The Supremes had 12 number 1 hits in the U.S. charts. Astonishing!

THE SUPREMES

The most famous female trio from the 1960s started as a quartet named The Primettes. Diana, Florence, Mary and Betty were four talented adolescents that got together in the Detroit housing project where they lived. They loved to sing, but when they got together to form a vocal group they could hardly imagine the fame that was to come. Betty left a year after they started and Barbara joined by then. Barbara was still able to record an album with the famous *Motown* label, but she too had to leave in 1962. The Supremes were now a trio and they had a whole team of composers and producers working for their voices. Some other singers came and left, but this trio was the most successful one for longest. They topped the charts and they rivaled The Beatles!

BAND MEMBERS

Diana Ross

Florence Ballard

Mary Wilson

Betty McGlown

Barbara Martin

FORMED IN 1959

ORIGIN Detroit, MI

GENRE Soul, R&B, Pop, Disco

FAMOUS SONGS

Baby Love

Stop! In the Name of Love

You Keep Me Hangin' On

You Can't Hurry Love

JAMES BROWN

If Ray Charles is the father and Sam Cooke the inventor then James Brown was the godfather of *Soul*. He wrote more than 800 songs and influenced artists from all kinds of music genres while creating a new one at the same time: *Funk*. Popular music communicates a lot through rhythm and nobody did it better than James Brown. He oozed energy in his live act: it looked like he was battery-powered and he could even do the splits in midair. James Brown had a lot of nicknames: "Hardest Working Man in Show Business;" "Mr. Dynamite;" "Soul Brother No. 1;" "The Godfather of Soul."

Young James Brown dreamt of becoming either a professional baseball player or a boxer.

DEBUT ALBUM 1959

ORIGIN Barnwell, SC

GENRE Funk, Soul, R&B

FAMOUS SONGS

Papa's Got a Brand New Bag; I Got You (I Feel Good);

It's a Man's World; Get Up (I Feel Like Being a) Sex Machine

His real surname was Gay but he added an "e" to it. Some say it was as a tribute to his hero, Sam Cooke, while others say it was to avoid being mistaken for his father.

MARVIN GAYE

Marvin Gaye started singing in church when he was 3 years old and then in several choirs later in his youth. He ended up learning how to play piano and the drums; music was the most important thing in his life. He even played on the streets, but at 21 he was hired by the most famous *Soul* label at the time, *Motown*, first as a drummer for other bands and then as a main artist. He became known as *Motown*'s Prince because he helped the label to turn into a hit factory.

DEBUT ALBUM 1961

ORIGIN Washington DC

GENRE R&B, Soul, Funk, Jazz, Pop

FAMOUS SONGS

Let's Get It On

I Heard It Through the Grapevine

What's Going On

Sexual Healing

STEVIE WONDER

Stevie Wonder was born blind, but that did not stop him from becoming a star even as a child. By 10 he was able to play the drums, bass guitar, piano and harmonica, and by 12 he had already released a record. His success lasted for decades. His song *I Just Called to Say I Love You* was a huge success and topped the charts in many countries. Stevie Wonder sang duets with many famous singers: Paul McCartney, Lenny Kravitz, Celine Dion, Michael Jackson, Whitney Houston, Beyoncé, Ariana Grande and more.

I just called to say I love yooou!

Stevie Wonder is so inspiring that he once said: "Just because a man lacks the use of his eyes doesn't mean he lacks vision!"

DEBUT ALBUM 1962

ORIGIN Saginaw, MI

GENRE Soul, Pop, R&B, Funk, Jazz

FAMOUS SONGS

Superstition

You Are the Sunshine of My Life

I Just Called to Say I Love You

The Rolling Stones covered some of Otis's songs (That's How Strong My Love Is and Pain in My Heart) and he responded in kind by recording his own version of (I Can't Get No) Satisfaction.

DEBUT ALBUM 1964

ORIGIN Dawson, WI

GENRE Soul, R&B

FAMOUS SONGS

(Sittin' on) The Dock of the Bay

These Arms of Mine

I've Been Loving You Too Long

OTHER MUSICIANS
be all ears

THE DRIFTERS
Stand By Me
This Magic Moment

NINA SIMONE
My Baby Just Cares for Me
Feeling Good

WILSON PICKETT
In the Midnight Hour
Mustang Sally (popularized by)

IKE & TINA TURNER
A Fool in Love
River Deep-Mountain High

AL GREEN
Take Me to the River
Let's Stay Together

SLY AND THE FAMILY STONE
Dance to the Music
Everyday People
Thank You

CURTIS MAYFIELD
Move On Up
Superfly

PARLIAMENT-FUNKADELIC
(I Wanna) Testify
One Nation under a Groove

OTIS REDDING

When Otis Redding was a child he entered many talent shows. He was so talented that he was asked to not do it anymore, so that others could have a chance of winning. Otis dropped out of school when he was 15 because his father got sick and he had to help his mother out. He worked as a well driller, gas station attendant and *Gospel* singer in a church to help out the family. His career was very short because he died when he was only 26, yet he managed to record 6 albums in 4 years. He had a wonderful voice and sang in a very profound way. His biggest hit, the song *(Sittin' on) The Dock of the Bay*, was recorded shortly before he passed away and was only released after his death, becoming an instant hit.

OLD TRADITIONS, NEW GUITARS

Until singer and guitarist Woody Guthrie – and later Bob Dylan – appeared on the scene, *Folk* was the name given to traditional music made by communities and passed through oral tradition from one generation to the next. Guthrie innovated by combining inspiration from the melodies of those old songs with his own rebellious and intimate lyrics. Later, a young and talented fan of Guthrie, a musician who went by the name Bob Dylan, was inspired by his work and added a pinch of *Rock*, creating a new genre along the way –

Folk Rock. In this category you can also find Simon and Garfunkel who are considered the greatest duo of the genre and also Joni Mitchell that, together with Joan Baez, is one of the main feminine forces of *Folk*.

LOOK OUT!

His real name was Robert Allen Zimmerman but he was so fond of Welsh poet Dylan Thomas that he "stole" his name.

The first Rock double album was Bob Dylan's Blonde on Blonde, released in 1966.

BOB DYLAN

Bob Dylan was one of the most important singers and songwriters of the 20th century. He learned how to play guitar and harmonica as a child and formed a band in high school. He then went on to study Arts at university but what he really enjoyed was playing music in clubs. His voice wasn't particularly good, yet he made up for it by writing incredibly beautiful and deep lyrics. Many

of his songs were true political poems and were adopted as civil rights and anti-war hymns, making Bob a voice for his generation. He demonstrated that we don't always have to be perfect to be good at what we do; we just need to be real. He won a lot of prizes, including 11 Grammys, a Golden Globe, an Oscar and a Pulitzer Prize. To the surprise of many, he even won the Nobel Prize in Literature in 2016.

DEBUT ALBUM 1962

ORIGIN Duluth, MN

GENRE Folk, Blues, Rock, Country, Gospel

FAMOUS SONGS

Blowin' in the Wind

The Times They Are a-Changin'

Like a Rolling Stone

OTHER MUSICIANS
be all ears

PETE SEEGER
If I Had a Hammer
Turn! Turn! Turn!

JOAN BAEZ
Diamonds & Rust
Silver Dagger

DONOVAN
Mellow Yellow
Sunshine Superman
Atlantis

VAN MORRISON
Brown Eyed Girl
Into the Mystic

BUFFALO SPRINGFIELD
For What It's Worth
Rock and Roll Woman

THE BAND
The Weight
Up On Cripple Creek

CROSBY, STILLS, NASH & YOUNG
Helpless
Our House
Teach Your Children

SIMON & GARFUNKEL

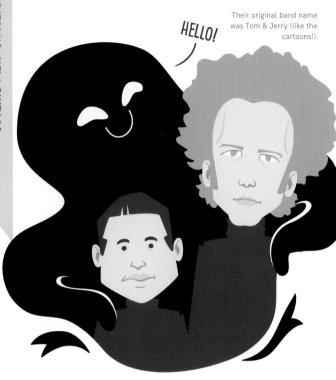

HELLO!

Their original band name was Tom & Jerry (like the cartoons!).

Paul and Art lived in the same neighborhood and went to the same school. In 1956 they started a duo and wrote some songs. They played in school parties and after a year they were able to gather enough money to release a single. It became a hit and got them on radio and TV. Not bad for a couple of 16-year-olds! This initial adventure lasted for a little over a year and then each of them went on with their studies and their music. By 1962 they got together again and released their first album as Simon & Garfunkel. Throughout the decade, they grew apart and rejoined several times. In 1970 they recorded their last album and, after having earned 6 Grammys, they split. Songs like *The Sound of Silence* or *Bridge over Troubled Water* became hymns for their generation, elevating them to the realm of the most influential musicians of all time.

BAND MEMBERS
Paul Simon
Art Garfunkel

FORMED IN 1956

ORIGIN Forest Hills, NY

GENRE Folk Rock

FAMOUS SONGS
The Sound of Silence
Mrs. Robinson
Bridge over Troubled Water
The Boxer
America

JONI MITCHELL

Joni had piano lessons when she was 7 but she gave up quickly: she could not play the songs she had in her head and found the compositions she had to learn boring. By 9 she was afflicted with poliomyelitis, a very serious disease, and she developed her artistic side while recovering. Through adolescence, she sang with friends and taught herself to play the guitar. By 20 she started to take music seriously and by 1968, when she was 25, she recorded her first album. Despite being considered one of the greatest *Folk* artists, Joni wasn't stuck to a single genre, getting inspiration from *Jazz*, *Rock* and *Pop*. The delicacy and deepness in her lyrics and music made her a source of inspiration for many artists up to this day.

DEBUT ALBUM 1968

ORIGIN Fort Macleod

GENRE Folk, Rock, Jazz, Pop

FAMOUS SONGS
Big Yellow Taxi
Both Sides
Now
The Circle Game
A Case of You

Her first love was painting. When she was 12 her English teacher inspired her to "paint with words," just like she did with the brush and it was then that her interest for poetry started.

By the early 1960s around Los Angeles, California, a new sport was making a splash, one where you rode waves by balancing yourself on top of a board – surfing was hip! This new sport brought along a new lifestyle and, it goes without saying, a new music genre, titled *Surf Rock*. Boards, beaches, the sea, cute girls and fast cars were the main themes behind the songs pioneered by Dick Dale but popularized by The Beach Boys.

Despite being part of the most famous Surf Rock band of all time, only one – Dennis Wilson – of the 5 members of the band knew how to surf.

THE BEACH BOYS

Brothers Brian, Dennis and Carl Wilson lived by the sea in California and from an early age loved to sing together in harmony, pretending to be in choirs. Their cousin Mike Love joined them, as well as a fellow American football player, Al Jardine; with the help of their parents they bought musical instruments and recorded a song. They became an instant hit.

Their harmonious voices and the fresh melodies Brian Wilson created showed that The Beach Boys weren't just another band, but actually one of the most important ones from the '60s. They were one of the few North American bands that continued to enjoy success after British bands like The Beatles and The Rolling Stones "invaded" the United States.

BAND MEMBERS
Brian Wilson
Dennis Wilson
Carl Wilson
Mike Love
Al Jardine

FORMED IN 1961

ORIGIN Hawthorne, CA

GENRE Rock, Pop, Surf, Psychedelic

FAMOUS SONGS
Surfin' U.S.A.
Good Vibrations
God Only Knows
California Girls
Wouldn't It Be Nice

OTHER MUSICIANS
be all ears

THE SHADOWS
Apache
The Rumble

DICK DALE & HIS DEL-TONES
Let's Go Trippin'
Misirlou

THE VENTURES
Walk Don't Run
Hawaii Five-O

THE SURFARIS
Wipe Out
Surfer Joe

THE TORNADOES
Bustin' Surfboards
Phantom Surfer

THE TRASHMEN
Surfing Bird
Malaguena

During the 1960s a vast group of British *Rock* and *Pop* bands became popular throughout Europe and the United States. Bands like The Beatles and The Rolling Stones but also The Animals, The Yardbirds and The Kinks were completely innovative, and a major influence on haircuts, fashion and style. When they became big across the globe, people called it the "British Invasion." Impressed by this creative explosion coming from Europe, a lot of American bands changed the way they played; by the end of the decade the style had spread out completely and influenced *Rock* and *Pop* all over the world.

The Beatles songs mention food quite often! Example include cornflakes, truffles, honey, octopus, turkey, marshmallows, strawberries, eggs, pepper, and pies!

THE BEATLES

John Lennon was in high school when he started his first band, The Quarrymen, soon being joined by Paul McCartney and George Harrison. After some name and member changes they finally found the right label, the right producer and the right drummer, Ringo Starr. After releasing the track *Love Me Do*, with its catchy melody, playful guitars and positive harmonies, The Beatles became huge. Their first album topped the UK chart for 30 weeks and was eventually knocked off by another one of their albums which stayed there for 21 weeks. They appeared in five movies and were known as "The Fab Four." There was even a word for the madness their fans showed: "Beatlemania." It was so strong that the concert-going fans screamed and cried and some even fainted. The band split in 1970 but the four members carried on with their solo careers. The Beatles still hold to this day the world record for most records sold – almost 300 million of them!

BAND MEMBERS
John Lennon
Paul McCartney
George Harrison
Ringo Starr

FORMED IN 1960

ORIGIN Liverpool

GENRE Rock, Pop, Psychedelic

FAMOUS SONGS
Love Me Do
Help!
Hey Jude
Let It Be
Yesterday

THE ROLLING STONES

Mick Jagger and Keith Richards went to primary school together, yet only became friends when they met again in adolescence. Mick Jagger already had a band and Keith joined it. Later on, Brian Jones joined as well and, after a few line-up changes, The

Did you know that Johnny Depp got his inspiration from Keith Richards when creating Captain Jack Sparrow in Pirates of the Caribbean? What a dead ringer!

Rolling Stones were finally formed. By 1964 the band started making a name for themselves, not just because of the music, but also for their rebellious attitude, in striking difference with The Beatles who were more clean-cut. In 1965, upon releasing the song *(I Can't Get No) Satisfaction*

they became superstars. The Rolling Stones' music was wild, and singer Mick Jagger's sensuality made them the band others wanted to hear or imitate. Because they played *Rock* strongly inspired by *Blues*, they paved the way for heavier genres like *Hard Rock*. The Rolling Stones

are the longest running active band. One of the secrets to their longevity may be Mick Jagger's good shape, as he continues to perform highly energetic concerts, singing and dancing non-stop. Every day he runs 5 miles, swims, rides a bike, practices yoga, pilates and ballet!

BAND MEMBERS

Mick Jagger

Keith Richards

Charlie Watts

Bill Wyman

Brian Jones

Mick Taylor

Ronnie Wood

Ian Stewart

FORMED IN 1962

ORIGIN London

GENRE Rock, Blues, Pop, Hard Rock, Psychedelic

FAMOUS SONGS

(I Can't Get No) Satisfaction

Paint It, Black

She's A Rainbow

Sympathy For The Devil

Angie

Start Me Up

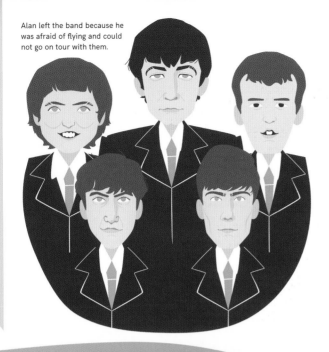

Alan left the band because he was afraid of flying and could not go on tour with them.

THE ANIMALS

The original members of the band (Eric, Alan, Chas, John and Hilton) got together in 1962 and became a sensation in their local live performances. They needed space to grow so they moved to London. By then the Beatlemania phenomenon was starting and The Animals seemed to fit perfectly the musical movement known as "British Invasion." It was common for bands to play songs from other musicians and have huge success. The Animals were no exception and made multiple covers. By 1964 they released their first album, which included the song *House of the Rising Sun* that jumped to the top of the charts everywhere and sold millions of copies. Some members left and others joined the band until 1966, when they changed their name to Eric Burdon and the Animals; the singer was the only original member left. By the end of the decade, they disbanded.

BAND MEMBERS
Eric Burdon
Alan Price
Chas Chandler
Hilton Valentine
John Steel
Dave Rowberry
Barry Jenkins
Danny McCulloch
John Weider
Vic Briggs
Andy Somers

FORMED IN 1962

ORIGIN Newcastle Upon Tyne

GENRE Rock, Blues, Folk, Psychedelic

FAMOUS SONGS
House of the Rising Sun
Don't Let Me Be Misunderstood

THE YARDBIRDS

In 1962 Keith and Paul were playing in a band called Metropolis Blues Quartet when Chris, Jim and Anthony joined them and changed the band's name to The Yardbirds. The quintet starting playing in bars in London and became the resident band at the *Crawdaddy Club* (replacing The Rolling Stones). Anthony was only 15 years old, so his parents didn't let him stay with the band, being replaced In 1963 by Eric Clapton as the main guitarist, still in time to see the success of the band exploding. Two years after Eric left he was replaced by another amazing guitar player, Jeff Beck, who then left a year later. By 1966 Jimmy (another guitar god!) replaced Paul on the bass and stayed there until 1968. The Yardbirds were the cradle from which three of the best guitarists in the world emerged—Eric Clapton, Jeff Beck and Jimmy Page!

BAND MEMBERS
Keith Relf
Jim McCarty
Chris Dreja
Paul Samwell-Smith
Eric Clapton
Jeff Beck
Jimmy Page
Anthony "Top" Topham

FORMED IN 1963

ORIGIN London

GENRE Rock, Blues, R&B, Psychedelic

FAMOUS SONGS
For Your Love
Heart Full of Soul

The Yardbirds shaped Rock, mixing in genres like Blues, Psychedelic and heavier Rock, using innovative techniques like feedback and distortion.

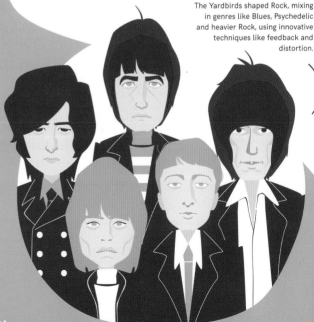

Pete left the band due to his claustrophobia; he was unable to be locked inside an airplane or recording studios.

They were forbidden from playing in the US for four years due to bad behavior.

THE KINKS

Brothers Ray and Dave were born into a large family where they were the only boys after six girls were born. They started to learn how to play the guitar from a young age (we've heard this story before, haven't we?) and organized their own improv bands at home. In 1964 The Kinks were born, coming from the garage to school dances and from school to the bars in town, adding band members Mick and Pete. That same year the song *You Really Got Me* was a smash hit with its raw and hard sound, placing the band on the musical map on both sides of the pond. Their throaty and wild sound would become the band's signature. Some say their music was the prototype for genres that would appear later, like *Hard Rock* and *Heavy Metal*. The music was "savage" and the artists themselves were quite naughty, especially the brothers, who were fighting all the time. Still, their songs were not just energetic, but also melodic and sweet. *Waterloo Sunset*, for instance, will go down in History as one of the best songs ever written. After calling it a day in 1996, they decided to get back together and record a new album in 2018.

BAND MEMBERS
Ray Davies
Dave Davies
Mick Avory
Pete Quaife

FORMED IN 1964

ORIGIN London

GENRE Rock, Pop

FAMOUS SONGS
You Really Got Me
Waterloo Sunset
Sunny Afternoon
Lola
All Day and All of the Night

OTHER MUSICIANS
be all ears

THE DAVE CLARK FIVE
Glad All Over
Because
Bits and Pieces

THE HOLLIES
Bus Stop
He Ain't Heavy (...)
The Air That I Breathe

HERMAN'S HERMITS
I'm into Something Good (popularized by)
No Milk Today

THE BYRDS
Mr. Tambourine Man (popularized by)
Turn! Turn! Turn! (popularized by)

SMALL FACES
Itchycoo Park
Lazy Sunday
All or Nothing

THE MONKEES
I'm A Believer
Last Train To Clarksville

THE TROGGS
Wild Thing
Love Is All Around

PSYCHEDELIC '60s

In the USA in the '60s, big changes were afoot: the war in Vietnam, the Moon landing, President Kennedy's assassination and the civil rights movement. Hippies began to be noticed more at this time. The Hippie movement opposed American society's beliefs and rules, creating a radically new lifestyle. Hippies used bright, extravagant clothing while exploring new sensations, in search of a peaceful and free life, closer to nature – that's where the term *Flower Power* comes from. This time, *Rock* shifted towards a more electrical and psychedelic path.

The line "I am the Lizard King. I can do anything," included on a Jim Morrison poem, got him the nickname Lizard King.

THE DOORS

Ray mastered the keyboards and was already in a band but after meeting Jim he wanted to play with him. Later on, John the drummer and Robby the guitarist joined too. The gloomy quartet known as The Doors was set. Jim Morrison was a very talented writer; the lyrics he wrote for the band were real poems. The 1967 track *Light My Fire* was their first of many major hits. They also had a lot of fans but they were the most controversial band at the time due to their unusual lyrics and Jim's live performances that were sometimes considered too daring. He was really unpredictable and provocative, which got him expelled from some concerts, and arrested by the police on stage! Some years after Jim's death, the remaining members recorded *An American Prayer* where they pieced together their music to poems Jim had recorded. They also put some poetry reading and music they had created together. The result is so moving that it's hard to believe it was made after Jim's death.

BAND MEMBERS
Jim Morrison
Ray Manzarek
John Densmore
Robby Krieger

FORMED IN 1965

ORIGIN Los Angeles, CA

GENRE Rock, Psychedelic, Blues, Hard Rock

FAMOUS SONGS
Light My Fire
Riders on the Storm
The End

Jim, Jimi and Janis didn't just share the first letter of their names; the three lived only 27 years.

Jimi Hendrix was able to play guitar with his teeth. Once, at a concert, he was so excited that he set his guitar on fire.

Janis Joplin was talented at karate – a black belt, no less!

JIMI HENDRIX

As with so many other rock stars Jimi Hendrix grew up in a tough family environment. In school, he was known for "playing the guitar" with a broom, yet his first real instrument was a ukulele which he found in the trash. Even with broken strings he tried to learn his first songs – his idol Elvis Presley's – on his own. He bought his first guitar when he was 15 and started practising every day, listening to his beloved artists, until he was good enough to become a backup musician to Little Richard and The Isley Brothers. In 1966 Jimi moved to London, where his talent got him noticed by several musicians. He created his band, The Jimi Hendrix Experience, which lasted only four years till his death, but managed to release three albums. He has gone down in history as one of the best guitar players of all time.

DEBUT ALBUM 1967

ORIGIN Seattle, WA

GENRE Rock, Psychedelic, Hard Rock, Blues, R&B

FAMOUS SONGS

Hey Joe

Purple Haze

The Wind Cries Mary

JANIS JOPLIN

Janis grew up in a small Texas city. As a child she used to sing in a church choir and started singing *Blues* and *Folk* as a teenager. She hated living in that city, with its constant oil-stink and prejudice against women who wanted to behave differently. She was rejected by other school girls for not caring that much about her looks and ended up preferring the company of boys who also enjoyed music. She went to the University of Texas, where she started playing small gigs. Her intense way of singing amazed her audiences; they hadn't seen any woman sing like that before. After living in many different cities, Janis found success in San Francisco, where she joined Big Brother and the Holding Company, a psychedelic band. After leaving the band Janis recorded two solo albums; her biggest success, *Pearl*, was released after her death.

DEBUT ALBUM 1967

ORIGIN Port Arthur, TX

GENRE Rock, Psychedelic, Blues, Soul

FAMOUS SONGS

Piece of My Heart

Cry Baby

Down on Me

Mercedes Benz

This band personified Psychedelic Rock through their songs, their outfits and their cover art. White Rabbit, their greatest hit, was inspired by Alice's Adventures in Wonderland and Through the Looking-Glass.

JEFFERSON AIRPLANE

BAND MEMBERS
Marty Balin
Paul Kantner
Grace Slick
Jorma Kaukonen
Jack Casady
Spencer Dryden

FORMED IN 1965

ORIGIN San Francisco, CA

GENRE Rock, Psychedelic, Folk, Blues, Pop

FAMOUS SONGS
Somebody to Love
White Rabbit

BAND MEMBERS
Jerry Garcia
Bob Weir
Ron "Pigpen" McKernan
Phil Lesh
Bill Kreutzmann

FORMED IN 1965

ORIGIN Palo Alto, CA

GENRE Rock, Psychedelic, Country, Folk

FAMOUS SONGS
Truckin'
Casey Jones

THE GRATEFUL DEAD

They started out as a Jug Band; they used odd instruments like jugs, kazoos and washboards to make music! This giant cauldron, where music was cooked with psychedelic seasoning, used a monstrous sound system. It weighed 75 tons and was made of 604 speakers that powered extremely loud concerts.

CREEDENCE CLEARWATER REVIVAL

Creedence appeared around Psychedelic Rock's heyday yet they were these down-to-earth lads with a knack for creating great songs closer to traditional American roots.

BAND MEMBERS
John Fogerty
Tom Fogerty
Stu Cook
Doug Clifford

FORMED IN 1967

ORIGIN El Cerrito, CA

GENRE Rock, Blues, Country

FAMOUS SONGS
Bad Moon Rising
Down on the Corner
Have You Ever Seen the Rain?

Reggae started in Jamaica in the late 1960s and rapidly became the country's dominant music genre. It has cool rhythms that derive from *Ska*. Despite being quite different from *Rock*, *Reggae* had a very special musician – Bob Marley – who was a huge influence on a lot of *Rock* musicians, and therefore we had to mention him. Artists like Jimmy Cliff and Peter Tosh, among others, were also very important in spreading *Reggae*.

Bob's favorite subject was math. He loved football and was a vegetarian.

The Clash were his fans and Eric Clapton recorded a cover of Bob's song I Shot the Sheriff which became a worldwide hit.

DEBUT ALBUM 1965

ORIGIN Saint Ann

GENRE Reggae, Ska

FAMOUS SONGS

Buffalo Soldier

Redemption Song

Is This Love

No Woman No Cry

BOB MARLEY

Bob was born in a small village in Jamaica. At 14 he and his family went to live in a poor suburb in the outskirts of Kingston, the country's capital. He was looking for inspiration in the music he heard both on the radio and played by local street artists. In the 1960s, pairing up with his friends Neville Livingston and Peter Tosh, he record-ed his first songs, which became popular only in his country. He lived in the USA and England, but went back home to Jamaica frequently. During the next decade, he rose to international fame with his band The Wailers. He recorded many albums and hits, touring all over the world. In Jamaica, Bob Marley was seen as a spiri-tual figure, sort of a poet and prophet, whose words were read and heard as if they were sacred texts. His lyrics speak about change, equality, revolution and injustice. Some of his songs are used as peace and love symbols. He has been considered one of the biggest artists of all time, having shared *Reggae* with the rest of the world.

OTHER MUSICIANS
be all ears

JIMMY CLIFF
The Harder They Come
Reggae Night

PETER TOSH
Legalize It
Bush Doctor

YELLOWMAN
Nobody Move, Nobody Get Hurt
Zungguzungguguzungguzeng

BURNING SPEAR
Slavery days
Old Marcus Garvey

THE SKATALITES
Guns of Navarone
Ska Ska Ska

Away from the heart of Hippie culture, some bands started out using inspiration from different cultural movements, like *Pop Art* or the *Mod* (as in modernist) movement. In the state of Washington, The Sonics' raw and direct music helped create *Garage Rock*; in London, The Who broke guitars and tried to "rupture eardrums" in the audience; in New York, The Velvet Underground went with an avant-garde image, driven by the bohemian and intellectual vision of the visual artist Andy Warhol. Other bands like The Stooges, Television and MC5 would pave the way for *Punk* which was just around the corner.

THE VELVET UNDERGROUND

Young Lou Reed was only 22 when he met John Cale in New York. Both loved music and were classically trained but John was more into avant-garde music and Lou was hooked on poetry. They formed The Velvet Underground with two other artists, and started playing in art galleries and poetry readings. In 1965 they met Andy Warhol who invited them to his artistic projects and paired them up with Nico, a German singer. The result was so good they recorded an album with her: *The Velvet Underground and Nico.* Their music was ahead of its time, creating a weird feeling for listeners. This record – but also the band itself – was recognized as a major work of art that took *Rock* to uncharted territories. Lou Reed then pursued an important solo career that you'll get to know further ahead.

The cover for their first album was drawn by Andy Warhol and was known as "the banana album."

OTHER MUSICIANS
be all ears

THE SONICS
Psycho
Strychnine
Boss Hoss

THE MONKS
Shut Up
Oh, How to Do Now

LOVE
Seven & Seven Is
Alone Again Or

MC5
Looking At You
Kick Out the Jams

SUICIDE
Ghost Rider
Dream Baby Dream

THE MODERN LOVERS
Astral Plane
Roadrunner
I'm Straight

TELEVISION
Venus
Marquee Moon
The Dream's Dream

BAND MEMBERS
Lou Reed
John Cale
Sterling Morrison
Maureen Tucker

FORMED IN 1964

ORIGIN New York, NY

GENRE Rock, Art Rock, Punk, Experimental, Avant-garde

FAMOUS SONGS
I'm Waiting for the Man
Sunday Morning
Venus in Furs
Sweet Jane
Rock & Roll

Do you know the CSI TV series? Opening credits songs Who Are You, Won't Get Fooled Again and Baba O'Riley are from this band!

They got into the Guinness Book of Records for being the loudest band, but that record stopped being measured because more and more people started having hearing problems after attending concerts.

THE WHO

Pete and John were schoolmates and played together, first *Jazz* then *Rock*. John got into a band called Detours in which Roger was also a member and Pete was invited to play the guitar. Later Keith joined too – he was a one-of-a-kind drummer! In early 1964 they found a name: The Who. By the end of the year they changed their style and their concerts became more violent. Ever since they debuted their first single on TV, smashing a guitar and kicking the drums, they became famous and their music reached the general public. They were the pioneers of *Opera Rock* and one of the first *Rock* bands to successfully use synthesizers.

🇬🇧

BAND MEMBERS
Roger Daltrey
Pete Townshend
John Entwistle
Keith Moon

FORMED IN 1964

ORIGIN London

GENRE Art Rock, Hard Rock, Punk, Psychedelic, Pop

FAMOUS SONGS
My Generation
Substitute
Baba O'Riley
Who Are You

THE STOOGES

The Stooges got together in 1967, but only started playing for real after Iggy Pop attended a concert by The Doors. He was so impressed with Jim Morrison that he got inspired to act crazy on stage too. By the late '60s and early '70s the band became a sensation but only for a limited audience; they were too raw, noisy and dangerous for the general public. After releasing three unsuccessful albums they disbanded, but over the next decades, they became a cult band, paving the way for *Punk*. Iggy Pop, on the other hand, pursued a solo career and became a symbol for *Rock*, always playing topless. His best-known songs *Lust for Life*, *Candy*, and *The Passenge*r can still be heard on the radio.

Peter Jackson, the director of The Lord of the Rings trilogy, used Iggy Pop's body as source of inspiration for Gollum.

They took their name – The Stooges – from a group of comedians that used that name.

🇺🇸

BAND MEMBERS
Iggy Pop
Ron Asheton
Scott Asheton
Dave Alexander

FORMED IN 1967

ORIGIN Ann Arbor, MI

GENRE Rock, Punk, Garage Rock, Hard Rock

FAMOUS SONGS
I Wanna Be Your Dog
Raw Power
Gimme Danger
Search and Destroy

ELECTRIC SYMPHONIES

By the late '60s and early '70s, a new music style was developing. It was inspired initially by *Psychedelic Rock* but drew some ideas from avant-garde music such as *Classical*, *Jazz* and *Experimental*. Song structure is more complicated and you'll find that in some of these *Progressive Rock* albums every track contributes to a complete story (creating what is called a "concept album"). Terms like *Art Rock* and *Progressive Rock* or simply *Prog Rock* are used to describe music that bands like King Crimson, Genesis, Pink Floyd, Yes, Jethro Tull, and Emerson, Lake & Palmer created.

Their 1988 Delicate Sound of Thunder album
was the first Rock record to be played in space!

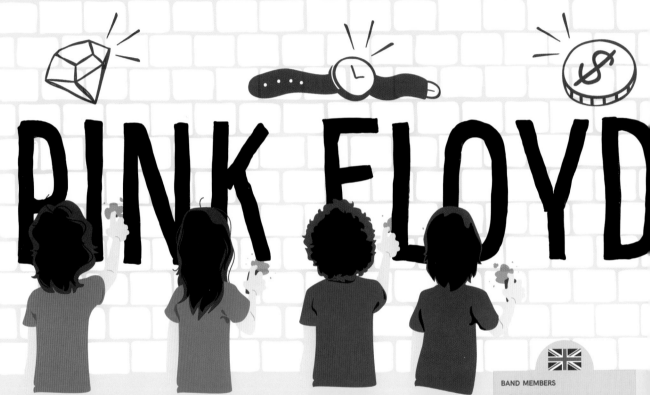

PINK FLOYD

In early 1964 three architecture students – Roger, Nick and Richard – banded with an art student, Syd, and started playing *R&B* for their college mates. After three years they had developed their own psychedelic sound, to which they added from other genres: heavier *Rock* but also *Classical*, *Prog*, *Blues*, *Folk* and *Electronic*. They recorded their first album *The Piper at the Gates of Dawn* at Abbey Road, a studio in London (coincidentally, The Beatles were recording an album called *Sgt. Pepper's Lonely Hearts Club Band* on the other side of the studio). By their second album David Gilmour joined in, ending up substituting Barrett. In 1973, they released *The Dark Side of the Moon*, an album that catapulted them to the top as one of the biggest *Rock* bands ever. It is one of the best-selling worldwide albums and stayed in the *Billboard* Chart for 917 weeks (until 1988)!

BAND MEMBERS

Roger Waters

Nick Mason

Richard Wright

Syd Barrett

David Gilmour

FORMED IN 1965

ORIGIN London

GENRE Progressive Rock, Art Rock, Psychedelic, Blues, Hard Rock

FAMOUS SONGS

Wish You Were Here

Another Brick in the Wall

Comfortably Numb

GENESIS

Peter, Tony, Michael and Anthony were schoolmates when they started their first band. In 1967, they chose the name Genesis. After their first two albums, Anthony left the band and Phil Collins and Steve Hackett joined. During their 8 initial years, Genesis were considered a cult band. They created elaborate *Art Rock* and gave a strong contribution to the foundations of *Prog Rock*. By 1975, Peter Gabriel, who was very theatrical, decided to leave the group and Phil Collins, almost unintentionally, took on singing duties. Fans were not fond of this change, but the band reached new heights as the new line-up shifted to more romantic *Pop* songs. In their solo careers, Peter Gabriel and Phil Collins became superstars.

BAND MEMBERS
Tony Banks
Mike Rutherford
Phil Collins
Peter Gabriel
Steve Hackett
Anthony Phillips

FORMED IN 1967

ORIGIN Blackpool and Luton

GENRE Progressive Rock, Art Rock, Pop, Rock

FAMOUS SONGS
Supper's Ready
The Musical Box
Tonight, Tonight, Tonight
I Can't Dance

Their debut album was titled From Genesis to Revelation (the first and last books of the Bible) which made record stores place it in the religious section. Because of this, only 650 copies were sold – an extremely low number!

KING CRIMSON

King Crimson were formed in 1968 when Robert – a multi-instrumentalist boy who was also a guitar virtuoso – and drummer Mike abandoned the Giles, Giles and Fripp trio and banded with three other musicians: Greg Lake, Ian McDonald and Pete Sinfield. The band acquired quite a stockpile of instruments, including wind instruments like saxophones, flutes and clarinets, but also keyboards: clavichords, pianos, organs, vibraphones, and a new electronic instrument, the Mellotron, a pioneer in sampling techniques. *In the Court of the Crimson King*, their first album, is still the one most beloved by fans and, according to those in the know, a true *Prog Rock* manual.

...ert Fripp wrote the opening melody for ...dows Vista. He is the only original band ...mber: to this day, 21 musicians have been ...he band!

BAND MEMBERS
Robert Fripp
(only constant member)

FORMED IN 1968

ORIGIN London

GENRE Progressive Rock, Art Rock

FAMOUS SONGS
Epitaph
Starless
The Court of the Crimson King

OTHER MUSICIANS
be all ears

THE MOODY BLUES
Go Now
Nights in White Satin
Tuesday Afternoon

PROCOL HARUM
A Whiter Shade of Pale
A Salty Dog
Conquistador

JETHRO TULL
Aqualung
Thick as a Brick
Locomotive Breath

YES
Close to the Edge
Owner of a Lonely Heart

RUSH
Tom Sawyer
Limelight

CAMEL
Stationary Traveler
Rajaz

EMERSON, LAKE & PALMER
Lucky Man
Fanfare for the Common Man

MIKE OLDFIELD
Tubular Bells
Moonlight Shadow

THE ALAN PARSONS PROJECT
The Raven
Eye in the Sky
Don't Answer Me

SUPERTRAMP
The Logical Song
Dreamer
Cannonball

Within these pages you'll find the bands that coined the label *Hard Rock*, even though they were not the first ones trying out heavier sounds: The Rolling Stones, The Who, The Kinks, Jimi Hendrix and others had already taken the first steps toward a massive guitar sound. Still, it was with Led Zeppelin and Deep Purple that *Hard Rock* rose as a music genre that would open the gates to heavier branches of *Rock*, like *Heavy Metal*, and which influenced younger bands like Guns N' Roses, whom you'll find here as well.

LED ZEPPELIN

In 1966 guitar player Jimmy Page joined The Yardbirds, but by then the band was so tired of touring that they ended up disbanding. Jimmy was determined to start his own band and after searching for a while he found the perfect musicians to create Led Zeppelin. The band became known by the genre they helped create – *Hard Rock* – but mixed together the best of the '60s, from *Blues* to *Folk*. Their style was typical '70s: bell-bottom pants, long hair and shirts with extravagant patterns and lots of colors. Nearly everyone who starts learning how to play the guitar ends up playing *Stairway to Heaven* – it's almost mandatory but not easy at all! It's a beautiful song that changes from quiet, ballad-like parts to others dominated by heavy guitars.

BAND MEMBERS
Jimmy Page
Robert Plant
John Paul Jones
John Bonham

FORMED IN 1968

ORIGIN London

GENRE Hard Rock, Blues Rock, Folk Rock

FAMOUS SONGS
Stairway to Heaven
Whole Lotta Love
Kashmir

Their lyrics touch on literature, mythology and philosophy. Did you know that they even sang about The Lord of The Rings?

OTHER MUSICIANS
be all ears

STEPPENWOLF
Born to Be Wild
Magic Carpet Ride

NAZARETH
Hair of the Dog
Love Hurts (cover)

TWISTED SISTER
We're Not Gonna Take It
I Wanna Rock

VAN HALEN
Ain't Talkin' Bout Love
Jump!

JOURNEY
Don't Stop Believin'
Open Arms

BOSTON
More Than a Feeling
Don't Look Back

WHITESNAKE
Fool for Your Loving
Here I Go Again

DEF LEPPARD
Let's Get Rocked
Pour Some Sugar on Me

BON JOVI
Livin' on a Prayer
Wanted Dead or Alive

DEEP PURPLE

This band had a lot of members but their musical adventure started with guitarist Ritchie, singer Rod, bassist Nick, keyboardist Jon and drummer Ian. During the initial years and their first three albums, Deep Purple's sound was soft and influenced by *Blues* and *Progressive Rock*, yet in the early '70s everything changed – including two members. Ian Gillan and Roger Glover joined and the band's sound became a lot heavier. By 1972, with their album *Machine Head* and the song *Smoke on the* *Water*, Deep Purple won their place in the history of *Rock*.

You may have never heard of Deep Purple before but for sure you've heard their most famous song: Smoke on the Water. Any self-respecting guitarist learns how to play this one!

Deep Purple were known for playing so loud that they broke a Guinness Record, which was then topped by The Who.

BAND MEMBERS
Ritchie Blackmore
Jon Lord
Ian Paice
Rod Evans
Ian Gillan
Nick Simper
Roger Glover

FORMED IN 1968

ORIGIN Hertford

GENRE Hard Rock, Heavy Metal, Blues Rock, Progressive Rock

FAMOUS SONGS
Speed King
Smoke on the Water
Highway Star

ALICE COOPER

Vincent Furnier was born in Detroit but grew up in Phoenix, where he started his first band at the age of 16. They went through different names and styles until, in 1969, the group chose the name Alice Cooper and moved to Los Angeles. They started to get well-known, especially because of their crazy concerts which included pillow fights, guillotines, electric chairs, snakes, fake blood... the perfect set for a horror movie. This type of show was used on purpose to shock the public. They did it so well that Vincent earned the nickname The Godfather of *Shock Rock*. In 1975 the band broke up, but Vincent decided to keep the name for himself. Throughout his long career he still found the time to become a skilled golfer, a restaurant owner, actor and radio host.

Alice Cooper has run for President of the USA in every election since 1972. He does it for the laughs, but he also uses the opportunity to take a few shots at politicians.

DEBUT ALBUM
1969 (with Alice Cooper Band)
1975 (solo)

ORIGIN Detroit, MI

GENRE Hard Rock, Heavy Metal, Glam Rock

FAMOUS SONGS
I'm Eighteen
School's Out

ZZ TOP

The three members of ZZ Top were born in 1949 and started their band when they were 20, in 1969. They are the longest-running constant line-up American band. Billy, Dusty and Frank loved *Rock* and *Blues*, yet mixed those styles in a heavy, intense way and came down in history as one of the biggest *Hard Rock* bands. Their style is quite unique: *Country* suits, dark shades and, of course, Billy and Dusty's famously long beards. They say they started growing them long in the mid-70s.

The only band member that does not have a beard is... Frank Beard. He already has it in the name so he doesn't need one!

BAND MEMBERS
Billy Gibbons
Dusty Hill
Frank Beard

FORMED IN 1969

ORIGIN Houston, TX

GENRE Rock, Blues Rock, Hard Rock

FAMOUS SONGS
La Grange
Legs
Sharp Dressed Man

AC/DC

Their eccentric lead guitarist Angus Young was known for his schoolboy-uniform stage outfit and for his frenetic dancing across the stage.

Brothers Malcolm and Angus Young moved from Scotland to Australia and formed AC/DC in 1973. In the beginning they presented themselves as a *Glam Rock*-influenced band, but with some member changes the band found the right line-up: Bon Scott sang, the Young brothers played guitar, Mark Evans (and later Cliff Williams) played bass, and Phil Rudd played the drums. Their mix of powerful beats, heavy rhythms and raspy voice with a theatrical stage presence showcased a heavier AC/DC. After becoming famous in their home country and crisscrossing Europe, they finally hit the big-time in the US with the album *Highway to Hell* and a lot of miles on the road! In 1980 the band suffered a tragic loss with Bon's death and were on the verge of giving up when they found their new voice in Brian Johnson. Throughout the '80s, '90s and first half of the 2000s they were constantly successful.

BAND MEMBERS
Angus Young
Cliff Williams
Phil Rudd
Malcolm Young
Bon Scott
Mark Evans
Dave Evans
Brian Johnson

FORMED IN 1973

ORIGIN Sydney

GENRE Hard Rock, Blues, Rock

FAMOUS SONGS
Highway to Hell
Thunderstruck
You Shook Me All Night Long

...rosmith were the first [roc]k band to appear on an [epi]sode of The Simpsons.

AEROSMITH

BAND MEMBERS
Steven Tyler
Tom Hamilton
Joey Kramer
Joe Perry
Brad Whitford

FORMED IN 1970

ORIGIN Boston, MA

GENRE Hard Rock, Blues Rock, Glam Rock

FAMOUS SONGS
Walk This Way
Janie's Got a Gun
Livin' on the Edge
Crazy

The history of Aerosmith started in 1970 when Steven Tyler (that guy with a mouth even bigger than Mick Jagger's) saw guitarist Joe Perry play with his band. Aerosmith was started and they hit the road and the record button, releasing their first album in 1973. Their career had ups and downs but these bad boys were able to produce a lot of records and world famous hits, from agitated *Rock and Roll* anthems to weepy ballads. Aerosmith are the all-time best selling *American Hard Rock* band, with more than 150 million records sold worldwide.

Before learning how to play the guitar Slash was a BMX bike rider and even participated in professional tournaments.

GUNS N' ROSES

For the first two years of existence they toured a lot and their concerts became infamous for their violence. In 1987 they launched *Appetite for Destruction* and, once the single *Sweet Child O' Mine* appeared on the music channel MTV, sales went through the roof and their fan base grew a lot. Guns N' Roses were not fine young men and early in their career gave back some of *Rock*'s rawness, dirtiness and violence. By the early '90s the band broke music charts with the release of *Use Your Illusion I* and *II*. The music videos created for album tracks like *Don't Cry* and *November Rain* were among the most expensive made until then, and became popular everywhere. The audience soon lost interest: with Axl and friends' rock star excesses and the appearance of *Grunge* – a style radically different from what Guns N' Roses played – they were never to return to the explosive strength of their beginnings. Still, they continue to be a well-respected band and Slash is among the best guitarists in the world.

BAND MEMBERS
Axl Rose
Slash
Izzy Stradlin
Duff McKagan
Steven Adler

FORMED IN 1985

ORIGIN Los Angeles, CA

GENRE Hard Rock, Heavy Metal

FAMOUS SONGS
Welcome to the Jungle
Sweet Child O' Mine
Paradise City
November Rain

What do these musicians have in common? They started their careers around the same time; were highly influential in the history of *Rock*; are admired by generations of fans, musicians and artists from other areas who were inspired by them; pursued solo careers, despite playing in bands too; are consummate musicians who wrote and performed; have connections to literature, cinema and other art forms and are loved by the general public as well as by the alternative crowd. They were also capable of creating songs that made us swirl on the dance floor or cry due to their beautiful melodies. Are they the only ones? No, but you have to admit they look really nice all together!

It looks like his eyes have differ colors but that's because he has permanently dilated pu

His song Space Oddity was used British television during the M Landing in 1

DAVID BOWIE

David Bowie is known as the chameleon of rock and you'll shortly understand why. When he was 13 he played the saxophone, and by 16 he was already playing in bands. He recorded his first album by the age of 20, and two years later released a worldwide hit called *Space Oddity*. From one record to another, David changed both his musical as well as his vi-sual style until, in 1972, he showed just how special he was by releasing *The Rise and Fall of Ziggy Stardust and the Spiders from Mars*. At that time he pretended to come from the future and dressed accordingly. During the '70s he went through a lot of genres, in-cluding *Glam Rock, Mod, Funk, Soul, Electronic* and *Krautrock*. In the '80s he continued to move with the times, reaching the whole planet with the hits-filled album *Let's Dance* which we still hear on the radio. He also tried out *Electronic* and *Industrial* music in the '90s and kept surprising audiences un-til the last days of his life. He transformed his ap-pearance like a chameleon, changing with the tide, set-ting trends and new paths in music. Besides being a music star he was also an actor, record producer and guest artist for other musi-cians.

DEBUT ALBUM 1967

ORIGIN London

GENRE Art Rock, Pop, Glam Rock, Electronic, Experimental

FAMOUS SONGS

Heroes

Space Oddity

Modern Love

Life On Mars?

Let's Dance

Rebel Rebel

Fame

China Girl

BRUCE SPRINGSTEEN

Bruce fell in love with *Rock* when he saw Elvis Presley playing on TV. When he turned 16 his mother borrowed some money to buy him a guitar. By the late '60s he was already playing in bars with several bands and it was around that time he met the musicians of his current ensemble, the E Street Band. Springsteen is loved for his humble roots and down-to-earth manner, and these are reflected in the complex personalities, urban romances and rebel spirit in his songs; audiences from all ages can identify with this. Bruce is known for his deep and husky voice. He and his band are also famous for their long, marathon-like concerts. It is still common for them to play for 3 or 4 hours non-stop!

Springsteen is known as The Boss because at the end of each concert he used to collect payment in cash and share it with the band members.

DEBUT ALBUM 1973

ORIGIN Long Branch, NJ

GENRE Rock, Folk, Rock and Roll

FAMOUS SONGS

Hungry Heart

Born in the U.S.A.

Glory Days

Dancing in the Dark

NEIL YOUNG

Nirvana's Kurt Cobain and Pearl Jam's Eddie Vedder have always been Neil Young fans. Flannel shirts are their trademark.

Disease and his parents' divorce marked Neil's childhood. He sought refuge in music and started to learn how to play the banjo and the ukulele. By the mid-60s he founded Buffalo Springfield, a *Folk* band, and by the end of the decade released his first solo album. For the following record he played with a band he had worked with for many years, Crazy Horse. He joined the trio Crosby, Stills & Nash, adding his surname "Young," and played with them at the mythical Woodstock Festival, in 1969. During the next couple of decades he stuck to *Folk* and *Country*. His use of feedback, the distortion in his guitar sound, and the fury he poured into his music seduced a new generation that by the '90s followed his footsteps, giving rise to *Grunge* and naming him their godfather. Neil continued experimenting and delighting his audiences with music both intense and soft, while defending Mother Nature whenever he had the chance.

DEBUT ALBUM 1969 (solo)

ORIGIN Toronto

GENRE Rock, Folk, Hard Rock, Country, Grunge

FAMOUS SONGS

Harvest Moon

Heart of Gold

Hey Hey, My My

Rockin' in the Free World

Before becoming a musician Tom worked as a doorman, a truck driver, a pizzeria employee, and served with the Coast Guard.

At one point Leonard Cohen studied Law to become an attorney. Lucky for us he changed his mind!

LEONARD COHEN

Leonard Cohen was born to a family that fostered his interest in arts from a young age, and he quickly fell in love with poetry and music. By 13 he was already playing the guitar and soon started singing and playing in Montreal bars. Those in the know say he did it to impress the girls! He published his first poetry book as soon as he finished his English Literature studies at university. Leonard only started his musical career after age 30, when a lot of labels said that he was too old to start. Still, he kept going and in 1967 released the album *Songs of Leonard Cohen* which already had all the trademarks of this deep-voiced troubadour, who sings about love, sex, religion and spirituality. That's how he did it until the end.

DEBUT ALBUM 1967

ORIGIN Westmount

GENRE Folk, Rock, Pop

FAMOUS SONGS

So Long, Marianne

Suzanne

Famous Blue Raincoat

I'm Your Man

TOM WAITS

Tom Waits learned how to play the guitar and the piano during high school; at age 22 he went to live in Los Angeles, where he started playing in bars. His songs were a mix of comic *Raps* and *Jazz* and *Blues* improvisations about stories that he heard on the streets. When he recorded his first album he was so broke that he had to sleep in his car or in really cheap hotels. Until the end of the '70s, his audiences were growing and he was earning more and more respect in the music community. He had used *Jazz*-related instruments but in the following decade he added marimbas and brass instruments to his wacky orchestra. Tom was an actor and wrote movie scripts and theatre plays, but is first and foremost an original musician: it's hard to forget that raspy, cavernous voice that tells funny and obscure stories about miserable and lonely characters with a wisp of *Blues*, *Folk* and *Jazz*.

DEBUT ALBUM 1973

ORIGIN Pomona, CA

GENRE Jazz, Blues, Pop, Rock, Experimental, Industrial, Folk

FAMOUS SONGS

The Heart of Saturday Night

Cold, Cold Ground

Innocent When You Dream

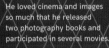

In the movie Harry Potter and the Deathly Hallows, Harry Potter and Hermione Granger dance to the sound of a Nick Cave song: "O Children".

He loved cinema and images so much that he released two photography books and participated in several movies.

LOU REED

Lou learned how to play the guitar by himself and played in several bands while in high school. He studied Cinema at university, and at 22 moved to New York to pursue a music career, spending some time writing songs for a label. By then he formed a band, The Velvet Underground (page 30). In 1970 he left the group and after two years released his first two solo albums. The first one sounded too much like his former band and wasn't successful, but the second one, *Transformer* (produced by his friend David Bowie), was not only highly successful but remains his landmark album, with well-known songs like *Walk on the Wild Side* and *Perfect Day*. Throughout his career, Lou recorded 16 albums of different genres and cultivated a rebellious personality which is why he's considered a precursor of *Punk*.

DEBUT ALBUM 1972

ORIGIN New York, NY

GENRE Rock, Experimental, Punk, Glam Rock

FAMOUS SONGS
Walk on the Wild Side
Perfect Day
Satellite of Love
Dirty Blvd.

NICK CAVE

Nick Cave was born in Australia, where he studied painting at university. In 1973 he met Mick Harvey with whom he started his first band, The Boys Next Door. They changed their name to The Birthday Party in 1980, becoming a cult band in Australia and Europe. After they split, Nick moved to Los Angeles and formed a new band – again with Mick Harvey – called Nick Cave and the Bad Seeds, being joined by Blixa Bargeld, from the German *Industrial* band Einstürzende Neubauten (page 74). Together they released 16 studio albums. Nick developed a unique sound by mixing *Blues*, *Gospel* and *Rock*, singing with his beautiful deep voice about religion, love, life and death. Despite being one of the biggest composers of the *Post-Punk* era, he still finds time to create new bands and write books and movie scripts.

DEBUT ALBUM 1984 (solo)

ORIGIN Warracknabeal

GENRE Post-Punk, Gothic, Experimental, Alternative Rock

FAMOUS SONGS
The Mercy Seat
The Ship Song
Straight To You
Do You Love Me?
Into My Arms

FEATHERS AND GLITTER

As you've probably noticed, there's often a connection between music and the way one dresses and acts. We touched on some musicians who impersonated characters on stage with props and special outfits to create an incredible show, like Peter Gabriel or David Bowie. Actually, the latter was part of the music (and fashion) movement that we're going to talk about now: *Glam Rock*. These artists used shocking outfits, (extremely) high heels, feathers, glitter, make-up and flashy hairdos. The bands below are examples within this movement, despite playing different music genres.

Mark was a poet and his spiritual and delicate lyrics were a joy for the fans. The name Bolan comes from the contraction of Bob and Dylan.

Roxy Music were one of the very first bands to create an elaborate visual style in their concerts, music videos and album covers.

T. REX

From a young age, Mark seemed to be born into stardom. In 1965, he recorded his first song, still influenced by *Folk* and *Psychedelic Rock*, and joined a band named John's Children, but got tired of it quickly. He had barely created his new group – Tyrannosaurus Rex – when they got their first gig. At the beginning, it was just Mark, with Steve on drums, but later the number of musicians grew. He changed the name, genre and look of the band. Their sound got more electrical and rock-oriented. Mark used eye-catching clothes, hats and feathers, and was a precursor for *Glam Rock*.

BAND MEMBERS
Marc Bolan
Steve Peregrin Took
Mickey Finn
Steve Currie

FORMED IN 1967

ORIGIN London

GENRE Glam Rock, Folk, Rock and Roll, Psychedelic

FAMOUS SONGS
Children of the Revolution
Get It On
I Love to Boogie

ROXY MUSIC

Ferry, Mackay and Eno admired modern art and fashion, and used those influences on Roxy Music. They added a lot of sophistication to *Glam* and future genres *Punk* and *New Wave* by combining this artistic side with an avant-garde image and electronic sound. Ferry was into *Soul* and *Pop*, while Eno was more into the idea of deconstructing *Rock*. With Eno's departure in 1974, the band started to revolve around Ferry and his voice, creating simpler, romantic melodies. After the band broke up, Ferry launched a solo career, becoming a symbol for elegance and Eno became one of the greatest music producers, leaving his mark on some of the best-known *Rock* and *Pop* artists.

BAND MEMBERS
Bryan Ferry
Phil Manzanera
Andy Mackay
Graham Simpson
Paul Thompson
Brian Eno
Eddie Jobson
John Gustafson

FORMED IN 1971

ORIGIN London

GENRE Art Rock, Pop, Glam Rock, Rock

FAMOUS SONGS
More Than This
Love Is the Drug
Do the Strand

QUEEN

Freddie studied Art and Graphic Design, John got a degree in Electronics, Roger became a bachelor in Biology and Brian achieved a PhD in Astrophysics!

BAND MEMBERS
Freddie Mercury
Brian May
Roger Taylor
John Deacon

FORMED IN 1970

ORIGIN London

GENRE Progressive Rock, Art Rock, Glam Rock, Hard Rock, Pop

FAMOUS SONGS
We Will Rock You
We Are the Champions
Bohemian Rhapsody
I Want to Break Free

Brian, Roger, John and Freddie started Queen in 1971, coming together from other bands. During the early years, still in college, they rehearsed and performed some concerts. In 1973 they released their first album and focused exclusively on their music, which then combined *Hard Rock*, *Prog Rock* and *Heavy Metal*. These were the genres of choice in the '70s but in the following years they mixed *Pop* with *Classical* and *Metal*. Success was right around the corner and it arrived with a 6-minute masterpiece called *Bohemian Rhapsody*. The song – which seems to cover all music genres, even *Opera* – topped the English music charts for nine weeks. It wasn't just the music that made the fans go wild; Freddie's vocal harmonies and exuberant style fuelled the fire. They released 14 studio albums until Freddie's death and collected hit after hit, transforming them into one of the biggest *Rock* bands in the world.

KISS

Kiss are a band with a strong image, wearing heavy make-up and cartoon-inspired outfits. Critics were unimpressed with their music (a mixture of *Rock*, *Hard Rock* and *Heavy Metal*) and exaggerated style, even after the release of several albums and many theatrical, pyrotechnics-heavy concerts. Still, their fan base kept getting bigger and bigger, and this kept the band performing.

BAND MEMBERS
Paul Stanley
Gene Simmons
Peter Criss
Ace Frehley

FORMED IN 1973

ORIGIN New York, NY

GENRE Hard Rock, Glam Rock

FAMOUS SONGS
I Was Made for Lovin' You
Detroit Rock City

OTHER MUSICIANS
be all ears

SUZI QUATRO
Can the Can
Devil Gate Drive

SLADE
Mama Weer All Crazee Now
Cum On Feel the Noize

SPARKS
This Town Ain't Big (...)
Barbecutie

THE SWEET
Block Buster!
The Ballroom Blitz
Hell Raiser

MOTT THE HOOPLE
All The Way From Memphis
Roll Away the Stone

NEW YORK DOLLS
Personality Crisis
Looking for a Kiss

Pop is a music genre that has one central aim: to produce hits. A hit is a song that sells a lot of copies. These songs are usually based on a formula: engaging rhythm, catchy melody and a chorus. Not all big hits have been produced by artists from this genre, but here you'll find heavyweight sales champions who are also the biggest stars in the *Pop* universe (and beyond). These artists have helped change the history of music while deeply influencing *Rock*! Their impact is so strong that – just like Elvis or The Beatles – they helped change the way people behave, dress and act.

He wore glasses as a teenager but didn't even need them – he just wanted to look like Buddy Holly

Robin and Maurice were twins. Barry is three years older.

ELTON JOHN

BEE GEES

Reginald Kenneth Dwight, better known as Elton John, started to teach himself the piano when he was 4. He was so talented that by 11 he won a scholarship to study at a music academy. By 17 he decided to dedicate himself full time to music; he started playing the piano in clubs and, later, wrote songs for other musicians. Before launching his solo career, he was in a band called Bluesology. In 1970 he got his first hit with a tune titled *Your Song*. His live performances included very extravagant clothes and accessories, feathers and truly original sunglasses. He used to say he did this because he sat and played the piano for two hours and had to find a way for people to look at him – and they did! Many other hits followed in his 50-year career where he tried out different music genres, wrote songs for stage and screen, won countless awards, sang with everybody and earned a unique spot in the history of music.

DEBUT ALBUM 1969

ORIGIN Pinner

GENRE Rock, Pop, Glam, R&B

FAMOUS SONGS

Your Song

Crocodile Rock

Rocket Man

Candle in the Wind

The brothers were born in the Isle of Man (British Isles) but soon moved to Manchester, where they started out in the music world. They were still children when they moved to Australia, where they became really popular, and started to get known as Bee Gees. Their admiration for The Beatles made them come back to England and adapt their music to the time's *Pop Rock*, experimenting with *Psychedelic* and *Prog Rock* a few years later. The trio would reach the top of the US and UK charts in 1967 with their *Soul*-inspired ballads. In 1975 they moved to the United States where Barry discovers the *falsetto* technique and, hopping on the *Disco* train, the Bee Gees became the biggest sensation of the genre. They may have been big in the 1960s, but by the late '70s and '80s they were giants who helped define *Pop* culture.

BAND MEMBERS

Barry Gibb

Maurice Gibb

Robin Gibb

FORMED IN 1958

ORIGIN Manchester

GENRE Pop, Soul, Disco, Rock

FAMOUS SONGS

Stayin' Alive

You Should Be Dancing

How Deep Is Your Love

Legend has it that Tina has the most beautiful and famous legs in the history of music.

Rod is a huge fan of Celtic F.C., a Scottish soccer team.

TINA TURNER

Anna Bullock was born with a fire in her belly but she did not have an easy childhood. When she was 11 her mother left and Anna moved from town to town, living with her grandparents and great-uncles and worked as a cleaning lady during her adolescence. In St. Louis she met her future stage companion, later husband, Ike Turner. Together they form an explosive duo, especially live. By this time Anna started to use the name Tina. After some successful years, Tina abandoned Ike because he didn't treat her well. She started again from scratch, alone and with very little money. Step by step she built her solo career and in 1984, with her *Private Dancer* album, Tina stormed the charts and showed that age (she was 45 at the time) means nothing when you have will and determination. After many awards and 200 million records sold, by 70 Tina was still performing electrifying concerts, with her powerful voice and high-heeled dance moves!

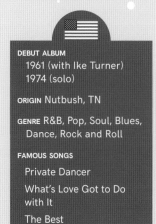

DEBUT ALBUM
1961 (with Ike Turner)
1974 (solo)

ORIGIN Nutbush, TN

GENRE R&B, Pop, Soul, Blues, Dance, Rock and Roll

FAMOUS SONGS
Private Dancer
What's Love Got to Do with It
The Best

ROD STEWART

When Rod was a young boy he had two passions: soccer and model trains. He wasn't able to follow his dream of becoming a professional soccer player, but had several jobs, travelled a lot and had many musical projects. Until the late 1960s, he was a member of bands like Steampacket, Jeff Beck Group and The Faces. His style was always in fashion; in the 60s, he dressed very neatly and combed his hair like a hedgehog (using his sister's hair gel) which, coupled with his raspy voice, became his trademark. Later he adopted a much wilder look, using leggings and leopard pattern. His bands played a mixture of *Rock*, *Folk* and *Blues* but his solo career had a softer style. The '70s and '80s were good for Rod, with a number of his songs becoming global hits. The next few decades, he concentrated on covering classics. He's a bestseller with over 100 million records sold!

DEBUT ALBUM 1969

ORIGIN London

GENRE Rock, Pop, Soul, Blues, Folk

FAMOUS SONGS
Maggie May
Young Turks
Baby Jane
Da Ya Think I'm Sexy

Billie Jean was the first music video from a black artist to be shown on MTV.

Michael Jackson made several dance steps famous, like the Moonwalk and the Robot.

MICHAEL JACKSON

Michael had 8 siblings with whom he shared a tiny house. The oldest three joined Michael and Marlon to create The Jackson 5. Their father quickly realized that Michael had a lot of talent for singing and dancing. By 1968 they landed a contract with the well-known label *Motown* and smashed the charts. By then, Michael was becoming so famous that he couldn't even go to school. When he launched his solo career he became a superstar. *Thriller* – his sixth album and biggest success – is the best-selling album of all time. This record brought one major innovation: music videos. Until then most videos used to promote songs simply showed the artists singing but Michael wanted to tell stories and even created short films, like the one for the song *Thriller*, which told a story about zombies. No previous artist had done what young Michael did: he changed the world of *Pop* music and proved that a young black singer could become the biggest music star in the world.

DEBUT ALBUM
1969 (The Jackson 5)
1972 (solo)

ORIGIN Gary, IN

GENRE Pop, Rock, Soul, R&B, Funk, Disco

FAMOUS SONGS

Beat It

Billie Jean

Thriller

Bad

Black or White

OTHER MUSICIANS
be all ears

TOM JONES
It's Not Unusual
What's New Pussycat?
She's a Lady

ABBA
Waterloo
Dancing Queen
Mamma Mia

BRYAN ADAMS
Cuts Like a Knife
Run to You
Summer of '69

BILLY JOEL
Piano Man
Uptown Girl
We Didn't Start the Fire

GEORGE MICHAEL
Careless Whisper
Faith
Freedom! '90

PET SHOP BOYS
West End Girls
Rent
Being Boring

CYNDI LAUPER
Girls Just Want (...)
True Colors

ALANIS MORISSETTE
You Oughta Know
Hand in My Pocket

SHERYL CROW
All I Wanna Do
If It Makes You Happy

ADELE
Chasing Pavements
Rolling in the Deep

Prince wasn't tall and always wore high heels because of that.

PRINCE

Prince Rogers Nelson got a knack for music from his parents and started composing when he was seven. He taught himself how to play piano, guitar and drums, and became a professional musician by 20. He had a very extravagant and provocative style. Prince created a genre called *Minneapolis Sound* mixing *Rock*, *Funk*, *Disco*, *R&B*, *Soul*, *Hip-Hop* and *Pop*, which made his music really danceable, and a strong influence for *Pop* throughout the '80s. Besides composing, singing and dancing, he produced and played lots (really, lots and lots!) of instruments: on his first 5 albums he played practically all of them. In his 30-year career he released 39 albums!

DEBUT ALBUM 1978

ORIGIN Minneapolis, MN

GENRE Rock, Funk, Pop, R&B, Soul

FAMOUS SONGS
Purple Rain
When Doves Cry
Kiss
Cream

MADONNA

Madonna was raised in a very religious family but soon revolted against the stringent rules. She was very rebellious, but she was also a straight-A student and a dedicated cheerleader. She was such a good dancer that she even got a scholarship to pursue dance studies at university. Until her solo career broke out, she sang and played drums in several *Rock* bands. She released singles and music videos and held concerts; tickets for her first tour were in such high demand that they had to move to larger venues. Her first songs showed Madonna as a *Punk*, and a sensual singer (fishnet stockings, lace gloves, headbands, underwear as outerwear and crucifixes around her neck), a style copied by adolescents around the world. Her popularity increased and she re-invented herself with every record she released. She was one of the most controversial artists in the '80s and '90s but is also an intelligent business woman: she got into the *Guinness World Records* as the best-selling female recording artist of all time, having sold over 300 million records.

DEBUT ALBUM 1983

ORIGIN Bay City, MI

GENRE Pop, Dance, Electronic, Rock

FAMOUS SONGS
Like a Virgin
Papa Don't Preach
Like a Prayer
Vogue

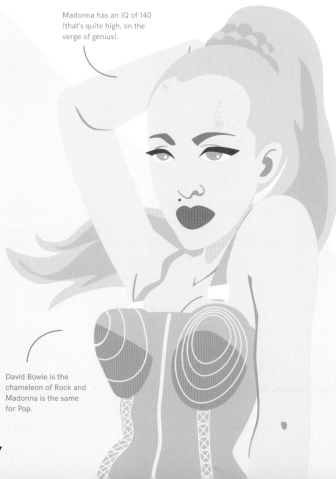

Madonna has an IQ of 140 (that's quite high, on the verge of genius).

David Bowie is the chameleon of Rock and Madonna is the same for Pop.

Glam Rock artists played existing music genres (with some innovations) and wore extravagant outfits and flashy make-up or accessories; however, in this category you'll find bands that had a stranger outlook and even stranger music. It's not easy to define these artists' genres, broadly speaking, as they are experimental and avant-garde which means they do not use popular formulas. It's as if they are unable to create a song without trying something that no one had done before.

Scientists from several fields celebrated Zappa by giving some animals his name: Amaurotoma zappa (a shellfish); Phialella zappai (a jellyfish); and Pachygnatha zappa (a spider).

Zappa even played such bizarre "instruments" as a bicycle and a car.

Kraftwerk are real-life hermits, rarely providing interviews. No one knows how to contact them.

FRANK ZAPPA

Frank was such a talented musician that even as a child he had already composed music for his school orchestra. He went through several bands, being a member of The Mothers of Invention for most of his career. He never followed a straight path typical of *Rock* bands but rather different ways, closer to *Jazz* and *Experimental* music. Many of his songs were parodies; sometimes he used scatological humor (topics considered obscene), and other times he talked about political or social issues and freedom of expression. He was obsessed with new technologies, and innovative in his usage of instruments and recording techniques. Frank had an irreverent style, with his distinctive moustache and shaggy hair. He showed up many times dressed in wacky ways with birds on his shoulder or a toilet paper scarf.

DEBUT ALBUM 1966

ORIGIN Baltimore, MD

GENRE Experimental, Jazz, Classical, Avant-garde, Progressive Rock, Art Rock

FAMOUS SONGS
Bobby Brown
Dancin' Fool
Montana

KRAFTWERK

Ralph and Florian met at Düsseldorf's Conservatory while learning classical music. Under the name Kraftwerk (power station), they started experimenting with everyday sounds and incorporating them in their songs. By the late '70s they dressed like store mannequins and played live with electronic instruments: keyboard, synths, drum machines, vocoder and instruments they invented or created. They were the pioneers of electronic music and the sounds and look we associate with robots.

BAND MEMBERS
Ralf Hütter
Florian Schneider

FORMED IN 1969

ORIGIN Düsseldorf

GENRE Electronic, Art Pop, Synth-pop, Avant-garde, Experimental

FAMOUS SONGS
Radioactivity
The Robots
The Model
Tour de France

THE RESIDENTS

Nobody really knows who The Residents are. It seems they travelled from their hometown of Shreveport, Louisiana, to the San Francisco Bay Area in the early '70s, but that's about it. The four band members never identified themselves, using only fictitious names, and appearing in public masked with giant eyeball helmets, top hats and tailcoats. Apparently starting out with no music training, they experimented with tape recorders and created some demos while they were assembling their studio. The band's interest in all things weird took them to crazy worlds like secret societies of moles, backstage at 'freakshows', atomic shopping carts, Eskimo lives, gingerbread men, Bible texts and tributes to The Beatles, The Rolling Stones and Elvis. The Residents' music is not easy to listen to because they use strange sounds and distorted voices. The fact of the matter is that they experimented with sounds no one had used before and wrote about worlds no one even dreamed about – while still creating beautiful songs.

BAND MEMBERS
Nobody knows who the Residents are. They are presented as "Randy", "Chuck", "Bob" and "Carlos".

FORMED IN 1969

ORIGIN Shreveport, LA

GENRE Avant-garde, Experimental, Art Rock, Electronic

FAMOUS SONGS
The Residents have no famous songs, so here are two suggestions: Aging Musician and I Hate Heaven.

Their first fan club – called W.E.I.R.D. (We Endorse Immediate Residents Deification) – had Matt Groening, creator of The Simpsons, as one of its members!

DEVO

The name Devo was inspired in the concept of "De-evolution" (they thought the human species was devolving instead of evolving). They released their first songs in 1977, showing their vision of society by mixing *Rock* with electronic sounds and robotic rhythms. Even though their first album was produced by Brian Eno they only reached mainstream success with the 1980 song *Whip It*. In live performance, they usually presented themselves with futuristic-looking yellow uniforms and yellow/red plastic cones on their heads.

Mark Mothersbaugh writes songs for TV programs such as Rugrats!

BAND MEMBERS
Gerald Casale
Bob Casale
Mark Mothersbaugh
Bob Mothersbaugh
Alan Myers

FORMED IN 1973

ORIGIN Kent and Akron, OH

GENRE New Wave, Synth-pop, Post-Punk, Art Pop, Electronic

FAMOUS SONGS
Whip It
Satisfaction (cover)
Mongoloid

OTHER MUSICIANS
be all ears

CAPTAIN BEEFHEART
Trout Mask Replica
Click Clack
Electricity

CAN
Vitamin C
Spoon
I Want More

NEU!
Super
Hallogallo

TANGERINE DREAM
Love On A Real Train
Phaedra
Stratosfear

DANIEL JOHNSTON
Speeding Motorcycle
Casper the Friendly Ghost

WEEN
Poop Ship Destroyer
Sarah

MR. BUNGLE
Squeeze Me Macaroni
Ars Moriendi

RAISE YOUR DEVIL HORNS!

This is one of the heaviest sections of the book. These musicians got their inspiration from artists that came before them and played heavier *Rock*, like Jimi Hendrix and Led Zeppelin. This new wave brought along heavier, faster and more violent sounds, allowed in part by technological advances in the construction of guitars, drums, pedals and amplifiers. Don't assume that *Metal* is just messy noise, though! It may surprise you to know that, amid the screams and artillery-like guitars and drums, there's precision and virtuosity comparable with *Classical* music orchestras! The music genre has spread out in many branches like *Thrash Metal*, *Death Metal*, *Black Metal*, *Speed Metal*, *Rap Metal*, *Nu Metal*, *Industrial Metal* and many others.

Black Sabbath were known as the first Heavy Metal band. Have you seen people that dress fully in black and are fans of zombie movies? If they lived in the '70s they might be Black Sabbath fans. Singer Ozzy Osbourne is known as the "Godfather of Heavy Metal."

IRON MAIDEN

Even though they scarcely appeared on the radio or television, Iron Maiden are one of most successful Heavy Metal bands of all time, having peaked in popularity during the '80s.

Eddie the Head is the band zombie mascot. He consistent appears on their album cove and in conce

They have fans everywhere, especially in Latin America.

BLACK SABBATH

BAND MEMBERS
Tony Iommi
Geezer Butler
Ozzy Osbourne
Bill Ward
Ronnie James Dio

FORMED IN 1968

ORIGIN Aston

GENRE Heavy Metal

FAMOUS SONGS
War Pigs
Iron Man

Black Sabbath are a heavyweight institution in England. They were *Heavy Metal* pioneers and from this band Ozzy Osbourne emerged: one of the most controversial characters in this music universe, with his vampire or devil-like figure. In 1970 they released two albums: *Black Sabbath* (which they recorded in just one day), and *Paranoid*, which is one of the most influential records in the development of *Heavy Metal*. They were innovative in their aggressiveness, dark-sounding name, lyrics on death and destruction, gothic style, pounding drums and harsh guitars, which many other bands copied and developed.

BAND MEMBERS
Steve Harris; Dave Murray; Paul Di'Anno;
Bruce Dickinson; Clive Burr; Adrian Smith;
Nicko McBrain; Janick Gers

FORMED IN 1975

ORIGIN London

GENRE Heavy Metal

FAMOUS SONGS Fear of the Dark;
The Number of the Beast

For 6 months Lemmy was Jimi Hendrix's roadie.

MOTÖRHEAD

Lemmy started to play *Rock and Roll* in 1964. Before creating Motörhead, he had gained a lot of experience as guitarist in Hawkwind, a *Psychedelic Rock* band from which he was fired. Shortly after, Motörhead was born.

They were the first *Metal* band to play fast and loud, almost like *Punk* before it even existed, paving the way for *Speed Metal* and *Thrash Metal*. Despite the numerous line-up changes,

Lemmy was always in the band and never stopped playing furious *Rock*.

BAND MEMBERS
Lemmy Kilmister
"Fast" Eddie Clarke
Phil "Philthy Animal"

FORMED IN 1975

ORIGIN London

GENRE Heavy Metal, Hard Rock, Rock and Roll

FAMOUS SONGS
Overkill
Hellraiser
Ace of Spades

OTHER MUSICIANS
be all ears

JUDAS PRIEST
Painkiller
Victim of Changes

MANOWAR
Blow Your Speakers
All Men Play On 10

ANTHRAX
Madhouse
I Am the Law

SLAYER
Raining Blood
Eyes of the Insane

SEPULTURA
Arise
Refuse/Resist

MEGADETH
Peace Sells
Symphony of Destruction

PANTERA
Walk
Cowboys From Hell

WHITE ZOMBIE
Thunder Kiss '65
Dragula

Metallica members throw large quantities of guitar picks to the audience in their concerts, resembling someone feeding pigeons.

METALLICA

James and Lars came from quite different backgrounds but had a shared

love for *Hard Rock* and *Heavy Metal*, fans of both Deep Purple and Motörhead. They found a lead guitarist and a bassist (after some trial and error) and started to write and record their initial songs.

The release of their first album was a turning point for *Metal*. The band was more complex, erudite and heavy, and they stood out from bands like Van Halen or, later, Bon Jovi. Their harder sound was welcomed by audiences who did not identify with those bands that played a more *Pop*-like *Metal*. The band's cult grew bigger and bigger, making them one of the most important ones in the genre and one of the biggest bands ever

BAND MEMBERS
James Hetfield
Lars Ulrich
Kirk Hammett
Cliff Burton
Jason Newsted
Robert Trujillo

FORMED IN 1981

ORIGIN Los Angeles, CA

GENRE Heavy Metal, Speed Metal, Thrash Metal

FAMOUS SONGS
One
Seek and Destroy
Nothing Else Matters
Enter Sandman

There are fewer famous women than men in *Rock*, but you'll find a lot of female artists throughout this book. These pages feature women only, and they're here together because they created music at the same time and inspired a lot of other women to choose *Rock* as a way of living. Their styles are quite different, but they share an innovative attitude and spirit.

Her 2010 memoirs won several important literature prizes.

JOAN JETT

DEBUT ALBUM 1980 (solo)

ORIGIN Los Angeles, CA

GENRE Hard Rock, Punk, Rock

FAMOUS SONGS

Cherry Bomb

I Love Rock 'n' Roll

Bad Reputation

PATTI SMITH

Patti was in high school when she fell in love with the arts, *Jazz* and *Rock*, participating in school plays and musicals. At 21, she moved to New York in the hopes of becoming a true artist; she got a job in a bookstore and got to know Robert Mapplethorpe, a visual artist who influenced her greatly. She used to recite poetry in quite an original way – accompanied by electric guitar. In 1974 she formed her own band and released the single *Piss Factory* which is considered by some critics as the first *Punk* song. Her first album was launched the following year and it was a huge success. This rocker poet changed the image of women in music, showing that there's no need to look like a model to be a *Rock* artist; you just need soul, originality and a guitar!

DEBUT ALBUM 1975

ORIGIN Chicago, IL

GENRE Punk, Rock, Art Rock

FAMOUS SONGS

Piss Factory

Because the Night

Dancing Barefoot

Joan got into the music world at 15 and became one of the most important women in *Rock*: she started two bands (The Runaways and Joan Jett & the Blackhearts) and a record label, and produced for all-female *Punk* bands that have their own movement (Riot Grrrl), like Bikini Kill or L7. Joan has several nicknames: "Queen of *Rock and Roll*," "Godmother of *Punk*" and "The First Riot Grrrl."

STEVIE NICKS

After performing a tap dance routine at a sixth-grade talent show Stevie decided to become an artist. She is known as a singer, songwriter and collaborator for the band Fleetwood Mac, which made her famous. Stevie pursued a solo career and was nominated 8 times for a Grammy, yet hasn't won any.

DEBUT ALBUM 1973

ORIGIN Phoenix, AZ

GENRE Rock, Pop

FAMOUS SONGS

(with Fleetwood Mac)

Dreams

Little Lies

(solo)

Talk to Me

I Can't Wait

CHRISSIE HYNDE

DEBUT ALBUM 1980

ORIGIN Akron, OH

GENRE Rock, New Wave, Punk

FAMOUS SONGS

Brass in Pocket

Don't Get Me Wrong

I'll Stand By You

Chrissie Hynde was one of the most influential women in Rock, especially in the '80s and '90s. She studied Arts and travelled to London, where she got acquainted with Punk in its infancy, and formed a band called The Pretenders. Chrissie is a vegetarian and animal rights activist. She hates fast food restaurants.

LAURIE ANDERSON

Laurie Anderson is a creative and free-spirited artist. Her work intrigues and hypnotizes the audience: she can write a symphony performed on automobile horns and then play the violin wearing frozen ice skates. Laurie is not just a singer. She's also a songwriter, dancer, movie director, music producer, photographer, poet, sculptress, ventriloquist, violinist, writer and tech fanatic (she invented a talking pillow!). She also works as an art critic in order to be able to do all of the above.

DEBUT ALBUM 1982

ORIGIN Glen Ellyn, IL

GENRE Avant-garde, Experimental, Art Pop, Electronic

FAMOUS SONGS

O Superman

Strange Angels

In Our Sleep

There's some dispute between Americans and Brits about where *Punk* started; some say it started in the USA, others in England. The seeds of *Punk* did in fact sprout in the US with bands like MC5, The Stooges, Velvet Underground and Patti Smith. The American branch was more musical and artistic; The Ramones were pioneers in limiting *Rock* to its bare essentials: four chords, simple melodies, shallow lyrics and fast pace. In England, unemployment and social injustice made disenchanted youths revolt, and express their anger through music. Attitude was key, and the first rule was there was no rules: to be a *Punk* was to break them. English band Sex Pistols shook British conservative standards by preaching chaos and anarchy in their songs and lyrics.

John Lydon (right) was known as Johnny Rotten because of his bad teeth.

OTHER MUSICIANS
be all ears

RICHARD HELL AND THE VOIDOIDS
Blank Generation
Love Comes in Spurts

BUZZCOCKS
Ever Fallen In Love
What Do I Get

THE DAMNED
New Rose
Love Song

NINA HAGEN
TV-glotzer
Superboy

THE CRAMPS
Human Fly
Garbageman

GENERATION X
Your Generation
Dancing with Myself

SEX PISTOLS

Sex Pistols were formed when Steve and Paul, from London's poor suburbs, started playing together. Glen, the bassist, joined later and Steve found a singer at Malcolm McLaren's boutique (McLaren was the band's manager). John Lydon was quite the character: he had green spiky hair and a t-shirt with "I Hate Pink Floyd" written on it. Malcolm convinced him to have a go at it right there at the store. John accepted and started singing and moving in a strange way. Everybody laughed but they also understood that despite the lack of vocal talent he was what they needed to express their thoughts. They started to play in clubs that allowed their violent music style and rude behavior. Audiences hated them, wherever they played, as most thought John couldn't sing, the musicians couldn't play and they all looked horrible. But then the single *Anarchy in the UK* broke out in 1976. Around that time, Glen left the band and was replaced by someone even crazier, Sid Vicious. Their song *God Save the Queen* shook England: the lyrics and the single cover were so provocative that they were considered very offensive to the British monarchy.

BAND MEMBERS
Johnny Rotten (John Lydon)
Steve Jones
Paul Cook
Glen Matlock
Sid Vicious (John Simon Ritchie)

FORMED IN 1972 or 1975 (arguable)

ORIGIN London

GENRE Punk, Rock

FAMOUS SONGS
God Save the Queen
Anarchy in the U.K.

RAMONES

In 1974, on the other side of the Atlantic, the Ramones got together. All band members used the surname Ramone despite none actually being family members or called that. The band found their followers in their initial concerts at *CBGB* (the temple of *Punk*), playing their simple and really fast *Rock and Roll*. It also landed them a contract for an album that became a real *Punk* "treatise" with hits like *Beat on the Brat* or *Blitzkrieg Bop*. The record has 14 tracks and runs just 29 minutes! Their four initial albums are the blueprint for *Punk*, especially the American variety (*Hardcore Punk*, for example), which you'll get to know in the next few pages.

BAND MEMBERS
Joey Ramone
Dee Dee Ramone
Johnny Ramone
Tommy Ramone

FORMED IN 1974

ORIGIN New York, NY

GENRE Punk Rock, Punk Pop

FAMOUS SONGS
Rockaway Beach
Blitzkrieg Bop
Sheena is a Punk Rocker

Most Ramones songs are around 2 minutes, partly because they don't play guitar solos.

THE CLASH

All the future members of The Clash had seen Sex Pistols play and agreed that was the type of *Rock* they wanted to play. Joe left his band (The 101ers) to join Mick, Paul and drummer Terry (later replaced by Nicky). On their first concert, in 1976, they had the privilege of opening for the Sex Pistols. They then followed them for the rest of the tour. They were starting to get quite well-known because they were seen as a dangerous band, even though that hadn't played that many concerts until then. Later, they got interested in political and social topics and their songs reflected that. The Clash were different from their peers because they had a concrete message and mixed *Punk* with other sounds, like *Reggae*, *Dub*, *Funk*, *Ska* and *Rockabilly*.

BAND MEMBERS
Joe Strummer
Mick Jones
Paul Simonon
Terry Chimes
Nicky "Topper" Headon

FORMED IN 1976

ORIGIN London

GENRE Punk, Rock, Reggae, Ska, Rockabilly

FAMOUS SONGS
Rock the Casbah
Should I Stay (...)
London Calling

The Edge, U2's guitarist, claimed that seeing The Clash live was a life-changing experience.

SMASH IT HARDER!

Beside music and attitude, *Punk* stood out also because of its sloppy fashion: torn jeans or skinny black trousers, leather jackets with metal spikes and studs, piercings, boots or tennis shoes, chains, spiked hair, mohawks, etc. Shortly after *Punk*'s first wave, *Hardcore*, a more radical version of the genre, appeared on the U.S. West Coast, especially in cities like San Francisco and Los Angeles. Bands like Black Flag, Dead Kennedys and Hüsker Dü created the movement, paving the way for a newer, more melodic generation of *Punks* like Bad Religion, Green Day and The Offspring.

Henry Rollins became a successful movie actor.

DEAD KENNEDYS

BAND MEMBERS
Jello Biafra
East Bay Ray
Klaus Flouride
6025
Ted
D.H. Peligro

FORMED IN 1978

ORIGIN San Francisco, CA

GENRE Punk, Hardcore Punk

FAMOUS SONGS
Holiday in Cambodia
California Über Alles

Dead Kennedys started out in San Francisco in 1978. For two years they played in clubs and concert halls in the Bay Area, inspired by British *Punk* and by Sex Pistols' provocative and revolutionary attitude. Political stands caused an impact – Jello criticized everyone and everything in the world of politics and had a special hatred for censorship and racism, using his lyrics to make fun of the situations he disapproved of. They became one of the first *Punk Hardcore* bands, with their fast playing (that also included *Surf* and *Rock*) and Jello Biafra's vibrating and raging voice.

BLACK FLAG

While the Ramones were kings of New York, their West Coast fans were creating a new twist on *Punk*: *Hardcore*. Black Flag were the first ones to do it. A decade and a half before it became popular to fuse *Punk* and *Metal*, Black Flag created this mix, adding humor to the recipe. They were more concerned with fast rhythms than melody. Through the years there were several line-up changes but

the band's heaviness and radical attitude remained the same. Henry Rollins, Black Flag's most famous member, ended up creating his own band called simply Rollins Band.

BAND MEMBERS
Greg Ginn (only original member)

FORMED IN 1976

ORIGIN Hermosa Beach, CA

GENRE Hardcore Punk, Punk

FAMOUS SONGS
Rise Above; My War

Jello Biafra ran for Mayor of San Francisco and even for President of the USA.

BAD RELIGION

Bad Religion was formed in 1979. Guitarist Brett created his own label (Epitaph) to release the band's records. Their first concert, in 1980, had almost no one in the audience and only after their first album did they start to gain notoriety in the *Hardcore* scene. Their sound changed somewhat through the years, becoming more melodic and incorporating guitar solos (which are quite unusual in *Punk*). Out of all the Californian *Hardcore* bands, Bad Religion was the one that lasted the longest.

BAND MEMBERS
Greg Graffin
Brett Gurewitz
Jay Bentley
Greg Hetson
Brian Baker

FORMED IN 1980

ORIGIN Los Angeles, CA

GENRE Punk Rock, Hardcore Punk

FAMOUS SONGS
We're Only Gonna Die
American Jesus
21st Century

OTHER MUSICIANS
be all ears

MISFITS
Last Caress
Attitude

BAD BRAINS
Banned in D.C.
I Against I

HÜSKER DÜ
Don't Want to Know (...)
Pink Turns To Blue

MINOR THREAT
Straight Edge
Minor Threat

MINUTEMEN
History Lesson – Part II
This Ain't No Picnic

OFFSPRING
Self Esteem
Pretty Fly (...)

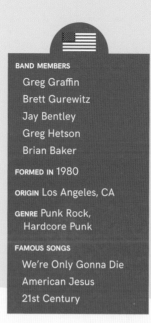

Despite their Punk attitude singer Billy Joe says he hates violence and that he would never hurt anyone.

GREEN DAY

Billie and Mike were best buddies in elementary school and it was Billie who taught his friend how to play the guitar. Instead of goofing around or playing sports they spent their days playing and coming up with songs. In high school they found a drummer and called themselves Sweet Children. By that time they had started hearing *Punk*. After many failed attempts at throwing a concert and nobody wanting to hear their demos they got acquainted with drummer John Kiffmeyer who accepted a spot in the band, and they changed its name to Green Day. In 1987 they finally played live for the first time, recorded their first songs and welcomed a new drummer, Tré Cool. With the 1994 release of their first album, *Dookie*, Green Day announced a new, more commercial generation of *Punk*. Everyone could now hear them on the radio, see them on MTV and watch as they won *Grammys*.

BAND MEMBERS
Billie Joe Armstrong
Mike Dirnt
John Kiffmeyer
Tré Cool

FORMED IN 1986

ORIGIN San Francisco, CA

GENRE Punk Rock, Pop, Rock

FAMOUS SONGS
Basket Case
When I Come Around
American Idiot

The bands that you'll get to know here share a common genre, *New Wave*, born out of *Punk* but adding fashion, art and a fascination for electronic sounds to *Punk*'s raw energy. It is musically diverse and begs to be danced to: from Blondie's *Pop-Disco* to Talking Heads' African rhythms-infused *Art Rock*, from The Police's *Rock-Reggae* to Madness' and The Specials' *Ska* revivalism, from Duran Duran's romantic *Synth-pop* to Depeche Mode's electronic *Synth-pop*. Many of these artists were very stylish and cared about their image. Debbie Harry was a fashion icon in New York, while the girls in The B-52's wore over-the-top hairdos and seemed to come out of a cartoon. The boys weren't in their shadow, either – they wore elaborate clothing and shaggy hair. This new religion had its own temple: New York club *CBGB*.

Debbie Harry started singing in a church choir.

BLONDIE

Upon graduating from art school, Debbie went to live in New York where she worked as a beautician and even as a Playboy bunny. By 1974 she met Chris Stein in the band The Stilettos and together they formed Blondie. With the line-up complete, the band started playing all the fashionable venues in New York. They celebrated *New Wave* by mixing in *Pop*, *Rock* and *Disco* with a rebellious attitude. Right about the time they released their first album, the *Punk* movement was bursting out and Blondie got associated with it as they played in the same venues as punks did. The band found this odd because in their minds they were playing *Pop*. The track *Heart of Glass* propelled them to success, which would last for a couple of decades. Debbie was really pretty and had a strong sense of style (she loved fashion!) and that's why she became a *Pop* icon, influencing the generation of women that followed.

BAND MEMBERS

Deborah Harry

Chris Stein

Clement Burke

James Destri

Gary Valentine

Frank Infante

Nigel Harrison

FORMED IN 1974

ORIGIN New York, NY

GENRE New Wave, Pop, Rock

FAMOUS SONGS

Call Me

One Way Or Another

Heart of Glass

Atomic

A "Talking Head" is someone who speaks directly to a video camera, as journalists do, for instance.

TALKING HEADS

David was born in Scotland and emigrated to the U.S. as a child. He met Chris and Tina at university and shared an apartment with them in New York. Talking Heads were born as a trio in 1975, a year in which they got to play at the hallowed club *CBGB* for the first time. Meanwhile, Jerry joined the band. Talking Heads brought something new to *Rock*: they had *Punk* energy, David's brainy and funny lyrics, African rhythms, *Funk* and *Art Pop* – ingredients that placed them squarely in the *New Wave* movement. Until its demise, the band was able to prove its versatility with experimental music, ethnic songs and *Pop* hits. Chris and Tina formed Tom Tom Club and David Byrne pursued a solo career, kept his interest in *World Music*, created a record label and exhibited his photography and design works.

BAND MEMBERS
David Byrne
Chris Frantz
Tina Weymouth
Jerry Harrison

FORMED IN 1975

ORIGIN New York, NY

GENRE New Wave, Art Rock, World Music, Punk

FAMOUS SONGS
Psycho Killer
Road to Nowhere
Life During Wartime
Once in a Lifetime

THE B-52'S

Fred, Keith, Cindy, Ricky and Kate decided to start a band while having dinner at a Chinese restaurant. They were happy and started to jam spontaneously, immediately naming the band The B-52's, a southern US slang word for a particularly exaggerated and piled-up beehive-like hairdo. Armed with their first single *Rock Lobster*, the band travelled up to New York and got to play the famous clubs. The number of fans outside the alternative circuit grew bigger and the band became *Pop* stars with their mix of *Garage Rock*, *New Wave* and playful attitude.

BAND MEMBERS
Fred Schneider
Kate Pierson
Cindy Wilson
Ricky Wilson
Keith Strickland

FORMED IN 1976

ORIGIN Athens, GA

GENRE New Wave, Rock, Pop, Garage Rock

FAMOUS SONGS
Love Shack
Rock Lobster
Good Stuff

Kate Pierson sang with Iggy Pop on the track Candy and with R.E.M. in Shiny Happy People. The B-52's recorded (Meet) the Flintstones for The Flintstones movie in 1994.

Sting got that nickname because of a black and yellow sweater that resembled a bee. His real name is Gordon Matthew Thomas Sumner.

THE POLICE

The Police were formed by the time *Punk* was making a splash in the music world. The band members came from very different backgrounds: Andy had played with The Animals and Soft Machine, and Stewart played with the *Prog Rock* band Curved Air. Sting, the singer, had various jobs and studied to become an elementary school teacher. In between jobs he played fusion *Jazz* with several bands. The Police's first album generated immediately two hits: *Roxanne* and *So Lonely*. They kept on composing successful tracks at every record they promoted. In a time where *Punk*'s sim-plicity and speed reigned supreme, The Police were adventurous by adding *Funk*, *Ska* and *Reggae* rhythms to *Rock*, making them a strong contender for leaders in the melting pot of genres named *New Wave*.

BAND MEMBERS
Sting
Andy Summers
Stewart Copeland

FORMED IN 1977

ORIGIN London

GENRE New Wave, Reggae, Rock, Funk, Ska

FAMOUS SONGS
So Lonely
Roxanne
Message in a Bottle
Walking on the Moon

DURAN DURAN

Schoolmates Nick and John formed Duran Duran in 1978, inspired by David Bowie and Roxy Music. Whilst working at the *Rum Runner* club in Birmingham (Nick as a DJ, John as a doorman) Duran Duran became the resident band and the club owners became their managers. They started to become really popular in the *Synth-pop* circuit (a more danceable version of *New Wave*), and were ready to launch their first record. The singles *Girls on Film* and *Planet Earth* dropped like bombs on the dance floors. Duran Duran were messengers of *New Wave* and *Synth-pop* for a wider audience, clev-erly using their glamorous image – they looked like fashion models – and music videos.

Duran Duran were Princess Diana's most beloved band.

BAND MEMBERS
John Taylor
Simon Le Bon
Roger Taylor
Nick Rhodes
Andy Taylor

FORMED IN 1978

ORIGIN Birmingham

GENRE New Wave, Pop, Synth-pop, Rock

FAMOUS SONGS
Girls On Film
Save a Prayer
Hungry Like the Wolf

Singer Dave Gahan stated that Johnny Cash's version of Personal Jesus was truer than the original one.

DEPECHE MODE

When Depeche Mode started in 1980 they were very much interested in all things electronic, like synthesizers and drum machines. This type of instrument became their trademark, as there weren't many bands at the time that almost exclusively used synths. They already had a legion of fans fol-lowing them in London's nightclubs when the time came for them to release their first album. It in-cluded the single *Just Can't Get Enough* which became a smash hit on the dance floors. The band was aligned with *New Wave* and *Synth-pop*, with its strong synthesized sound, somber and provocative *Pop* lyrics and the daring and seductive style of the musicians. Throughout the '80s Depeche Mode were the dominating force in electronic music for the masses, yet gradually they evolved a darker, more dramatic sound that made them one of the most suc-cessful alternative bands of their era. The 1990 knockout hit *Personal Jesus* was key to this, re-inforced by the fact that years later Johnny Cash chose it to create his own version of the song.

BAND MEMBERS
Dave Gahan
Martin Gore
Andy Fletcher
Vince Clarke
Alan Wilder

FORMED IN 1980

ORIGIN Basildon

GENRE Synth-pop, New Wave, Electronic, Alternative Rock

FAMOUS SONGS
Just Can't Get Enough
Personal Jesus
Enjoy the Silence
It's No Good

MELANCHOLIC ROCK

Bands in this genre heard a lot of *Punk*, which led to some of them forming. Out of this genre two others emerged: *New Wave*, (closer to *Pop* with a sprinkle of other styles), and *Post-Punk* (sadder, obscure, more introverted). Tied to it, another genre – *Gothic Rock* – was born, also in the late '70s. *Goth Rock* bands grew out of the strong ties they had with English *Punk* and *Post-Punk*, like Siouxsie and the Banshees, Joy Division, Bauhaus and The Cure.

Robert Smith does not have kids, but spoils his nephews and nieces. One day, he took them to Disneyland Paris and Minnie asked him for an autograph, which caught him by surprise!

SIOUXSIE AND THE BANSHEES

BAND MEMBERS
Siouxsie Sioux
Steven Severin
(only constant members)

FORMED IN 1976

ORIGIN London

GENRE Post-Punk, Gothic Rock, Alternative Rock

FAMOUS SONGS
Happy House
Spellbound
Peek-A-Boo

Susan and Steven met in 1975 and, despite a mutual taste for *Glam Rock*, were looking for something new – which they found in the Sex Pistols. Susan adopted the name Siouxsie and they formed Siouxsie and the Banshees. The band included Sid Vicious and Robert Smith. Siouxsie and the Banshees was one of the most important bands in the *Post-Punk* movement and helped to sow the seeds for *Gothic Rock*. Siouxsie Sioux's visual style – spiked hair and heavy make-up – was copied by many, even Robert Smith.

THE CURE

Robert's childhood may not have been particularly happy but in music he found a cure for the aches of his soul. At 17, he created Easy Cure (later The Cure) with his childhood friends Laurence and Michael. At first, their music was gloomy and melancholic, with strong guitars and intellectual lyrics. Despite having started as a *Post-Punk* band, The Cure reached worldwide fame: beautiful and sometimes sad lyrics written by Robert for tracks like *Lovesong*, *Pictures of You* and *Friday I'm In Love* catapulted the band to stardom in the late '80s and early '90s. Robert is the only original and permanent band member and is known for his white make-up, red lipstick and long, spiky hair.

BAND MEMBERS
Robert Smith
(only constant member)

FORMED IN 1976

ORIGIN Crawley

GENRE Post-Punk, Gothic Rock, Alternative Rock

FAMOUS SONGS
Just Like Heaven
Friday I'm in Love
Boys Don't Cry
Close to Me

JOY DIVISION

Just like in Siouxsie and the Banshees, two friends, Bernard and Peter were so impressed with a Sex Pistols concert that they decided to start their own band. They placed an ad looking for a singer, and Ian answered it. Stephen, the drummer, joined them the following year. They had a lot of fans before recording their first album, *Unknown Pleasures*, in 1979, because their concerts were pretty intense and the audience loved the melancholy that Ian transmitted through his voice and lyrics, as well as his disjointed dance moves. The following year the band toured and record-ed their second and last album, *Closer*, which Ian did not get to see. They became a cult band and the number of fans keeps growing. The rest of the band members formed New Order, which you'll get to know later on.

BAND MEMBERS
Ian Curtis
Bernard Sumner
Peter Hook
Stephen Morris

FORMED IN 1976

ORIGIN Manchester

GENRE Post-Punk

FAMOUS SONGS
Love Will Tear Us Apart
Transmission
Atmosphere

The famous cover for the album Unknown Pleasures represents the radio waves emitted by a pulsar, which is but the remains of a dying star that collapses on itself. Not exactly a joyful image, is it?

All band members have parallel projects, like Love and Rockets, which included all except Peter Murphy, who went on to pursue a solo career. Peter is known as the Godfather of Goth.

BAUHAUS

At its peak in the '80s, the band seemed to belong in a horror movie. Its music was also the perfect soundtrack: dissonant and ghoulish guitars, repetitive beats and a voice that seemed to come from beyond the grave. The first track, *Bela Lugosi's Dead*, was a 9 plus minute song inspired by horror movie star Bela Lugosi, the best-known cinema vampire. Even though other bands had used this style before, like Black Sabbath and Joy Division, Bauhaus were considered the first goth band, creating dark music and mysterious lyrics. In live performances they recreated a horror atmosphere with dark lights and coffins, while singer Peter Murphy impersonated a vampire.

BAND MEMBERS
Peter Murphy
Daniel Ash
Kevin Haskins
David J.

FORMED IN 1978

ORIGIN Northampton

GENRE Post-Punk, Gothic Rock

FAMOUS SONGS
She's in Parties
Bela Lugosi's Dead

The name of the band may have come from a breakfast cereal offer of a golden chain with an image of Jesus and Mary.

THE JESUS AND MARY CHAIN

Brothers Jim and William Reid really loved music and were always on the lookout for music genres coming from the UK and the US. While unemployed, they took the time to create songs and think about the band they wanted to become. After several failed attempts at being noticed by music labels and booking concerts in Scotland, their native country, the siblings moved to London. Their friend and fellow countryman Bobby Gillespie (from Primal Scream) gave them a hand (literally – he played drums in the band!), and eventually they were able to release their first single, *Upside Down*. At the beginning they were not very nice to the audience, as they played with their backs to them, which made concerts end in a big mess – the band broke their instruments and the audience destroyed the rest. Still, fans loved their songs, noisy as well as sweet and delicate, and music critics praised their first records. Even without a commercial hit, the artistic impact of the band was felt: their boys-against-the-world attitude, unruly hairstyle and black clothing, together with their very short concerts, heavy on feedback and sweet melodies, were inspiring to their fans.

BAND MEMBERS
Jim Reid
William Reid

FORMED IN 1983

ORIGIN East Kilbride (Scotland)

GENRE Post-Punk, Alternative Rock

FAMOUS SONGS
Just Like Honey
April Skies
Head On

OTHER MUSICIANS
be all ears

WIRE
Mannequin
The 15th

GANG OF FOUR
Damaged Goods
To Hell With Poverty!

THE PSYCHEDELIC FURS
Pretty In Pink
Love My Way

KILLING JOKE
Love Like Blood
Eighties

PUBLIC IMAGE LTD
This Is Not A Love Song
Rise

THE SOUND
I Can't Escape Myself
Winning

COCTEAU TWINS
Carolyn's Fingers
Heaven or Las Vegas

ECHO & THE BUNNYMEN
The Killing Moon
Lips Like Sugar

SISTERS OF MERCY
Lucretia My Reflection
This Corrosion

THE CHAMELEONS
Second Skin
Tears

DEAD CAN DANCE
Yulunga
The Host of Seraphim

MY BLOODY VALENTINE
Sunny Sundae Smile
You Made Me Realise

LOVE AND ROCKETS
So Alive
All in My Mind
Kundalini Express

THE THE
This Is the Day
Infected
Dogs Of Lust

FOLK PUNK

Both bands in this page have a lot in common: they love *Punk* and they love *Folk*. Seems weird, doesn't it? In fact, this *Punk* sound, mixed with traditional music, results in songs with a rebellious energy, vigorous instrumentals and folk joy. Violent Femmes, heavily influenced by *Country* and *Blues*, and The Pogues, coming from an Irish *Celtic* tradition, popularized a genre that shows that the history of *Rock* is made of blended sounds derived from different styles.

Brian Ritchie has more than 100 different musical instruments, which he used when recording the band's songs.

VIOLENT FEMMES

Brian and Victor were already playing in bands when they heard Gordon sing for the first time. Later on, Gordon showed that he was also a guitarist and a composer. The songs he created basically revolved around typical adolescent issues, but they were funny and intelligent. By 1981, it was common to hear them play in the streets of Milwaukee with an acoustic guitar, an acoustic bass guitar and a tranceaphone, a type of drum Victor invented. Once, they were playing in front of the *Oriental Theatre* club, where The Pretenders had a gig the same night. Guitarist James Honeyman-Scott heard the Violent Femmes and mentioned them to the rest of his band, who ended up inviting them to play at the end of the concert. With their first record came success, mainly because of the track *Blister in the Sun* (which became more notorious than the band itself).

BAND MEMBERS
Gordon Gano
Brian Ritchie
Victor DeLorenzo

FORMED IN 1980

ORIGIN Milwaukee, WI

GENRE Folk Punk, Folk Rock

FAMOUS SONGS
Blister in the Sun
Kiss Off
Add It Up

THE POGUES

Shane met Spider when he saw him play the flute in the London Underground and later found him again at a Ramones concert. Shortly after that they started singing Irish songs in London's streets and pubs, with James Fearnley playing the guitar. Three other musicians joined, and Shane started to write original songs. The sextet earned notoriety while touring with The Clash in 1984. That same year they released their first album, and by then they were already an octet! Some of them had to start singing backing vocals because Shane's voice could no longer make it. Sometimes you couldn't even understand the beautiful and poetic lyrics due to his alcohol abuse. He started to skip some concerts and ended up being fired from his own band.

BAND MEMBERS
Shane MacGowan
Spider Stacy
Jem Finer
James Fearnley
Cait O'Riordan
Andrew Ranken
Philip Chevron
Darryl Hunt

FORMED IN 1982

ORIGIN London

GENRE Folk Punk, Celtic Punk

FAMOUS SONGS
Fairytale of New York
Fiesta
Summer in Siam

Contrary to common wisdom, The Pogues are not Irish but rather from North London.

Ever since young Shane had teeth taken out by tying a string between them and a door handle, and slamming the door, he developed a fear of dentists and lost most of his teeth. Thankfully, he managed to fix them all!

During the '70s, Manchester had its share of successful bands, like Bee Gees, The Hollies and Herman's Hermits. The following decade saw the city being considered the main driving force behind the British alternative music, led by Joy Division (page 63), The Smiths and New Order. Some years later the success of bands that mixed *Psychedelic* and *Alternative Rock* with dance music generated a movement and gave the city a new nickname: "Madchester." You'll also find other Manchester bands throughout the book like Oasis or The Chemical Brothers.

Morrissey has been a vegetarian since his teenage years and convinced the rest of the band to stop eating meat. The song Meat is Murder begs the fans to become vegetarians themselves.

NEW ORDER

BAND MEMBERS
Peter Hook
Bernard Sumner
Stephen Morris
Gillian Gilbert

FORMED IN 1980

ORIGIN Manchester

GENRE Alternative Rock, Synth-pop, Post-Punk

FAMOUS SONGS
Blue Monday
Bizarre Love Triangle
Crystal

In the music video for the song Crystal the bass drum has "The Killers," a fictitious band name, written on it. Inspired by this video, nowadays there's a band with that name!

THE SMITHS

BAND MEMBERS
Morrissey
Johnny Marr
Andy Rourke
Mike Joyce

FORMED IN 1982

ORIGIN Manchester

GENRE Alternative Rock

FAMOUS SONGS
This Charming Man
Bigmouth Strikes Again
There Is a Light That (...)

Morrissey and Johnny met at a Patti Smith concert and noticed a lot of musical similarities between them, despite having very different personalities. Some time later, in 1982, Johnny showed up at Morrissey's house to convince him to start a band. Morrissey accepted. Drummer Mike and bassist Andy, joined and The Smiths were born. Two years later their debut album topped the music charts in the UK. The band's popularity grew with the release of two other hits-filled albums, yet tensions between Morrissey and Johnny led to the end of this band, who inspired so much of British *Rock* in the following decade. The Smiths became one of the most influential bands of all times, with its mixture on Johnny's magical guitar and Morrissey's suffering voice and heartbroken lyrics.

After Ian Curtis' death in 1980 there was no point in continuing Joy Division, yet the rest of the band were still eager to create music. Without Ian, the band was renamed New Order and changed its path: it mixed *Post-Punk* and *New Wave* aesthetics with electronic textures and dance rhythms, setting a new pace for England's music.

HAPPY MONDAYS

After forming Happy Mondays, brothers Shaun and Paul Ryder made a demo, and delivered it to the DJ at *Haçienda*, Manchester's best-known disco. Such a bold move earned them a contract with *Factory*, the label that released their first 4 albums (up to *Yes Please!*). This record led *Factory* to bankruptcy as Happy Mondays spent all the money somewhere other than recording the songs. The band bridged the gap between '80s Manchester alternative music and the emerging *Rave* dance scene that was growing in the UK. They mixed *Funk*, *Psychedelic* and *House*, pioneering the *Madchester* sound. Happy Mondays were also one of the first *Rock* bands incorporating *Hip-Hop* techniques in their songs: they weren't using samples, yet they shamelessly "stole" bits and pieces from other artists' melodies and lyrics.

BAND MEMBERS
Shaun Ryder
Paul Ryder
Mark Day
Paul Davis
Gary Whelan
Mark "Bez" Berry

FORMED IN 1980

ORIGIN Manchester

GENRE Alternative Rock, Electronic, House

FAMOUS SONGS
24 Hour Party People
Step On
Kinky Afro

Once, Shaun was so late to his concert that he rushed on stage at the wrong club, interrupting the concert of a band called Simply Red.

OTHER MUSICIANS
be all ears

THE FALL
C.R.E.E.P.
Mr. Pharmacist
Hit the North

A CERTAIN RATIO
Shack Up
Do the Du
All Night Party

THE DURUTTI COLUMN
Sketch for summer
Messidor

INSPIRAL CARPETS
This Is How It Feels
She comes in the Fall

SIMPLY RED
Money's Too Tight
Holding Back The Years

JAMES
Sit Down
Laid
Say Something
Sometimes

ELBOW
Friend Of Ours
Red
Powder Blue

THE CHARLATANS
The Only One I Know
One to Another

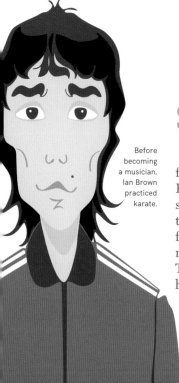

Before becoming a musician, Ian Brown practiced karate.

STONE ROSES

The band was officially formed when Ian, a young Punk/Hippie, joined his schoolmate John, a self-taught painter, and they found the musicians they needed to start playing. They performed in warehouses in the Greater Manchester area and started getting lots of fans. By early 1989 they were playing to packed houses in Manchester and London, and later that year they released their debut album, showcasing their interest in sounds from the '60s and a knack for electronic rhythms. The Stone Roses and their debut album are considered pioneers in the fusion of *Rock* culture and dance music.

BAND MEMBERS
Ian Brown
John Squire
Peter Garner
Mani (Gary Mounfield)
Reni (Alan Wren)

FORMED IN 1983

ORIGIN Manchester

GENRE Alternative Rock, Electronic, House

FAMOUS SONGS
She Bangs the Drums
I Wanna Be Adored
Waterfall
I Am the Resurrection

In this section you'll find the *Hip-Hop* masters that loved to mix it with *Rock*. Run-DMC and Beastie Boys pioneered a genre that came to be known as *Rap Rock*, followed by Public Enemy, who were not rockers in the full sense, yet filled with revolutionary attitude. They all featured heavyweight guests: Run-DMC with Aerosmith, Beastie Boys with Kerry King (one of Slayer's guitar players), and Public Enemy with Anthrax. Many artists, like Faith No More and Red Hot Chilli Peppers, took this fusion of *Rap* and *Rock* even further with the addition of *Heavy Metal*, paving the way for bands like Rage Against the Machine and System of a Down, who you'll read about further ahead.

Run-DMC were the first Rap group to appear on the cover of Rolling Stone magazine, have a song featured on MTV and go gold and platinum.

RUN-DMC

The members of Run-DMC grew up in a New York neighbourhood, sharing their love for music. Joseph's older brother, Russell Simmons, was a key figure in *Rap* and *Hip-Hop* labels, and with his help Joseph and Darryl started to *Rap*. Once they graduated from school they recruited their friend Jason to DJ for them. Their initial songs were really innovative, mixing *Rock* with *Hip-Hop* and introducing Joseph and Darryl's unconventional singing style; instead of alternating verses, they finished each other's sentences. Run-DMC made *Hip-Hop* a cultural and popular phenomenon, bringing hats, gold chains, and untied sneakers into fashion. The trio helped to pave the way for the second generation of *Rap*.

BAND MEMBERS

Joseph Simmons
Darryl McDaniels
Jason Mizell

FORMED IN 1981

ORIGIN New York, NY

GENRE Hip-Hop, Rap Rock

FAMOUS SONGS

It's Like That
King Of Rock
Walk This Way
It's Tricky

Public Enemy teamed up with Bomb Squad, a production team responsible for the creation of a sophisticated sound texture made up of siren sounds, scratches and bits of other songs.

PUBLIC ENEMY

Public Enemy got together at the university where Chuck studied and worked as a DJ at the college radio station, and where he met Hank from the Bomb Squad team and Bill Stephney from Def Jam Recordings. They all became friends quickly and had fun debating philosophy, politics and *Hip-Hop*. Inspired by the rhythms of Run-DMC, Public Enemy introduced a harsher, more intense sound that rewrote the rules for *Hip-Hop* and became the most influential and controversial *Rap* band in the late '80s. With his powerful and authoritarian voice, Chuck D raps about social issues, especially in the black community; Flavor Flav replies back with questions and provocations.

BAND MEMBERS

Chuck D; Flavor Flav;
Terminator X; Khari Wynn;
DJ Lord; Professor Griff;
S1W; The Bomb Squad

FORMED IN 1982

ORIGIN Long Island, NY

GENRE Hip-Hop, Rap Rock

FAMOUS SONGS

Rebel Without a Pause
Bring the Noise
Don't Believe the Hype
Fight the Power

In 1985 they were the supporting act in Madonna's tour. Her fans were so displeased with the band that they sighed in relief when she took the stage.

BEASTIE BOYS

Mike D, MCA and Ad-Rock were teenagers from well-off New York families when they formed Beastie Boys in the early '80s. Inspired by NY *Punk Hardcore*, the trio turned to *Rap* and *Hip-Hop*, teaming up with Rick Rubin, music producer and founder of Def Jam, a label specialized in *Hip-Hop*. The producer mixed their funny raps with Led Zeppelin's guitars, bits of *Metal* songs and sounds from TV programs. The band reached commercial success with their debut record, which was the first *Rap* album to reach #1 on the charts. At the end of the '80s the band matured and throughout the '90s they experimented to create hits with *Funk*, *Psychedelic* and *Soul*, keeping their adolescent charm and sensibility. They were the first popular all-white *Rap* group and their popularity reached unusual heights for three decades.

BAND MEMBERS
Mike D (Michael Diamond)
MCA (Adam Yauch)
Ad-Rock (Adam Horovitz)

FORMED IN 1981

ORIGIN New York, NY

GENRE Hip-Hop, Rap Rock, Punk, Alternative Rock

FAMOUS SONGS
Fight for Your Right
No Sleep till Brooklyn
Sabotage
Intergalactic
Body Movin'
Hey Ladies

OTHER MUSICIANS
be all ears

SUGARHILL GANG
Rapper's Delight

A TRIBE CALLED QUEST
Can I Kick It?

DE LA SOUL
Me, Myself & I
The Magic Number

N.W.A
Straight Outta Compton

CYPRESS HILL
Insane in the Brain
Boom Biddy Bye Bye

HOUSE OF PAIN
Shamrocks and Shenanigans
Jump Around

THE ROOTS
Distortion To Static
The Seed (2.0)

EMINEM
My Name Is
The Real Slim Shady

OUTKAST
Ms. Jackson
Hey Ya!

KENDRICK LAMAR
King Kunta
Humble

ALTERNATIVE NATION

You will find bands that are fairly different in this section; some are quite popular, others less so. Bands like U2 and R.E.M., who are nowadays considered commercial, were born from movements like *Post-Punk* and *College Rock*, in a time where the term "Alternative Rock" was used to classify bands such as these that did not fit the existing genres. We chose some that had (and still have) long careers that started back in the '80s and greatly influenced the music of the following decades. Some have reached the masses, like U2 or Red Hot Chili Peppers, while others maintain a more alternative audience, like Sonic Youth and Pixies.

Bono stated that Pop is different from Rock because Pop music tells us everything is alright while Rock says not all of it is ok, but it's possible to change it.

U2

U2 were formed when 14-year-old Larry placed an ad in school looking for musicians to start a band. The following hopeful young boys appeared at his doorstep: Adam Clayton, Paul Hewson (later called Bono Vox and after that simply Bono), and Dave Evans (The Edge). They rehearsed after school and at the weekends; soon a genuine bond and musical chemistry developed. And after rehearsing for more than a year they participated in a talent show where they won prize money and the opportunity to record their first demo. It didn't take long to go from a small group of followers to their first records, and with their fifth studio album their success reached stratospheric heights – and it's still growing strong. U2 have won the respect of musicians, critics and fans everywhere, by combining their unique sound with honest lyrics and a social and political message. Their melodic sound – based on the guitar textures created by The Edge and Bono's expressive voice – is immediately recognisable.

BAND MEMBERS
Bono
The Edge
Adam Clayton
Larry Mullen Jr.

FORMED IN 1976

ORIGIN Dublin

GENRE Alternative Rock, Post-Punk, Pop

FAMOUS SONGS
Sunday Bloody Sunday
Pride
With or Without You
One
The Sweetest Thing

Stipe says he can predict earthquakes: he feels a strong headache a few days prior.

R.E.M.

Michael was a shy little boy who loved *Punk*, but especially Patti Smith. By 1980 he formed R.E.M. with three friends and together they started to develop their own energetic blend of *Rock* and *Pop*. *Murmur*, their first album, was an instant hit, as it had all that was expected: beautiful guitar layers, passionate lyrics, atmospheric melodies and *Pop* hooks that would take them from college airplay to national radio. The '90s brought them two major successes: *Out of Time* (1991) and *Automatic for the People* (1992). R.E.M.

BAND MEMBERS
Michael Stipe
Bill Berry
Peter Buck
Mike Mills

FORMED IN 1980

ORIGIN Athens, GA

GENRE Alternative Rock, College Rock, Pop

FAMOUS SONGS
The One I Love
Losing My Religion
Shiny Happy People

were one of the first big *Alternative Rock* bands; with 15 albums under their belt (and despite their *Pop* sound) they kept their integrity, venturing into other music territories.

PIXIES

Black Francis split his youth between Los Angeles and Boston. Along the way he bought records at second-hand stores and listened to *Rock* on the *Jukebox* at his dad's bar. He met Joey in college and they started to write music together. In 1986 he quit his studies and travelled to Puerto Rico, where he was torn between flying to New Zealand to see Halley's Comet or forming a band. He and Joey ended up recruiting bass player Kim and drummer David. During their most innovative phase, between 1987 and 1991, they recorded 4 albums and one EP that, despite poor sales, have become quite influential and moved Pixies to *Alternative Rock*'s upper level. The band's sound, sometimes calm and soothing, and other times loud and heavy, became a blueprint for popular '90s *Rock* bands, including Nirvana.

Pixie is a type of fairy.

Kim Deal formed another band in 1990, The Breeders.

BAND MEMBERS
Black Francis
Joey Santiago
Kim Deal
David Lovering

FORMED IN 1986

ORIGIN Boston, MA

GENRE Alternative Rock, College Rock, Surf Rock

FAMOUS SONGS
Where Is My Mind?
Here Comes Your Man
Monkey Gone to Heaven
The Sad Punk

Black Francis' real name is Charles Michael Kittridge Thompson IV.

5

FAITH NO MORE

Bill, Roddy, James and Mike Bordin formed the band in the early '80s. At the beginning they didn't have a singer, so during their initial concerts they allowed audience members to sing. Chuck Mosley was a frequent volunteer and ended up joining the band but ended up being kicked out after two albums and two tours due to his unpredictable behavior. After writing new songs they needed a singer and they chose Mike Patton, who come from a bizarre band called Mr. Bungle. Mike wrote the lyrics to match the melodies, and that's how *The Real Thing* was born; it became their best-selling album. By fusing *Heavy Metal*, *Funk*, *Hip-Hop* and *Prog Rock*, Faith No More became a cult band.

BAND MEMBERS
- Chuck Mosley
- Mike Patton
- Mike Bordin
- Roddy Bottum
- Bill Gould
- James Martin

FORMED IN 1982

ORIGIN San Francisco, CA

GENRE Alternative Rock, Heavy Metal, Funk, Rap Rock

FAMOUS SONGS
- We Care a Lot
- Epic
- Midlife Crisis
- Everything's Ruined

Patton sings in countless bands, like Mr. Bungle, Tomahawk, Fantômas, Lovage, The Dillinger Escape Plan and Peeping Tom.

Patton's voice has the widest range know in the Rock and Pop universe: 6 octaves (imagine 42 white piano keys).

For a while the band played naked live, each one using only a sock to cover himself.

Blood Sugar Sex Magik was recorded at a mansion that had belonged to the famous magician Houdini.

RED HOT CHILI PEPPERS

Red Hot Chili Peppers were born out of the friendship that bonded Anthony, Flea and Hillel in high school. The trio, heavily influenced by *Funk* and California *Punk*, started to rehearse with drummer Jack Irons, with whom they perfected their sound and stage presence. By the end of the '80s, and with two new members joining – John Frusciante and Chad Smith – success came with their fourth album and stardom with the fifth, *Blood Sugar Sex Magik*, a smashing 1991 hit. By tearing down musical barriers, they became one of the most original bands around, thanks to Anthony's various vocal styles (spoken word, rap, singing), Frusciante's melodic and emotional guitar, and Flea's electric bass, which in his hands became a major instrument. The recipe for success came from the fusion of their talent as musicians and the explosive mix of *Funk*, *Rock* and *Rap*, allowing them to sit on the throne since then.

BAND MEMBERS
- Anthony Kiedis
- Flea
- Chad Smith
- John Frusciante

FORMED IN 1983

ORIGIN Los Angeles, CA

GENRE Alternative Rock, Funk, Rap Rock

FAMOUS SONGS
- Give It Away
- Under the Bridge
- Scar Tissue
- Can't Stop

SONIC YOUTH

Thurston Moore enjoyed a different, dissonant kind of *Rock* (one that sounds a bit off-key) and he moved to New York, where there were others playing that kind of music (*No Wave*). He started playing with his girlfriend, Kim, and together they formed the first version of Sonic Youth. During the first five years they played with Lee Ranaldo and several drummers. Their early recordings were rough, drenched in feedback and alternative tunings, as they positioned them-

Thurston Moore and Kim Gordon were married in 1984 and divorced in 2011.

In 1985 Sonic Youth created a band called Ciccone Youth, in honour of Madonna.

In 1999 the truck that had all of their musical gear was stolen. Most of it was unique instruments that had been heavily modified by the band.

selves against *Pop* music, which is easy to listen to. Later, they integrated more traditional and melodic sounds in their music. In the mid-80s they became a cult phenomenon, and in 1986 they hired drummer Steve Shelley. From there till the band's demise, Sonic Youth became an *Alternative Rock* institution and invented a new sonic landscape that has rede-fined what a *Rock* guitar can do, constantly finding uncharted music territory. They were present in key moments during the last three decades of the history of *Rock*: in the *Post-Punk* revolution of the '80s, in the innovative '90s *Rock* and in the 2000s revivalism, proving that the importance of a band is measured by its influence and not by the number of records sold.

BAND MEMBERS

Kim Gordon
Thurston Moore
Lee Ranaldo
Steve Shelley

FORMED IN 1981

ORIGIN New York, NY

GENRE No Wave, Noise Rock, Alternative Rock, Post-Punk

FAMOUS SONGS

Teen Age Riot; 100%; Sugar Kane; Incinerate

OTHER MUSICIANS
be all ears

BUTTHOLE SURFERS
Who Was in My Room Last Night?
The Wooden Song

PRIMAL SCREAM
Loaded
Movin' on Up
Damaged
Rocks

THE FLAMING LIPS
She Don't Use Jelly
Do You Realize?
Yoshimi Battles (...)

DINOSAUR JR
Freak Scene
Get Me
Out There
Feel the Pain

YO LA TENGO
From a Motel 6
Deeper into Movies
Mr. Tough

JANE'S ADDICTION
Jane Says
Been Caught Stealing
Stop!
Just Because

LEMONHEADS
It's a Shame about Ray
Confetti
Into Your Arms

Welcome to *Industrial Rock*, the heaviest section of the book. If you think about *Industrial* music, it's only natural that you imagine factories and machines, and that wouldn't be too far from the truth. One of the first bands to explore this genre used work tools like hammers and metal objects to create sounds. The first wave of industrial bands – like Throbbing Gristle or Einstürzende Neubauten – started out as performance art. The second generation had bands like Skinny Puppy or KMFDM who added dance melodies, while the American band Ministry added *Metal* guitar riffs, and Nine Inch Nails created more traditional songs that allowed them to reach a wider audience in the late '80s and early '90s.

The band's name can be translated as "Collapsing New Buildings."

Al once lost a bet with his daughter Adrienne; he had to get 16 piercings on his face, all at once.

EINSTÜRZENDE NEUBAUTEN

Young Blixa enjoyed tearing apart tape recorders and experimenting with musical instruments. In 1980, he accepted an invitation to play in a Berlin club but only chose the musicians to play with him after being invited. Those initial band members joined him not just for the concert but also for the next four decades. With *Kollaps*, their debut album, they declared war on conventional music. They were highly original, making their own instruments from metallic sheets, drills, hammers and found objects. Einstürzende Neubauten were pioneers in the *Industrial* genre by mixing noisy guitars, screams, noise and hellish rhythms. You can't wait to hear it, right?

BAND MEMBERS
Blixa Bargeld
N.U. Unruh
F.M. Einheit
Mark Chung
Alexander Hacke

FORMED IN 1980

ORIGIN Berlin

GENRE Industrial, Avant-garde, Experimental

FAMOUS SONGS
Yu Güng, Feurio!
Haus der Lüege
Stella Maris

MINISTRY

Al was born in Cuba but moved to the US as a young child. He lived in many different cities and worked as a DJ, forming Ministry in 1981. This band is considered one of the pioneers of the *Industrial* genre (with *Metal* and dance music thrown into the mix) and if you hear them you'll notice they are really heavy. It's funny to notice their initial songs were very melodic and danceable – very *New Wave* – but that changed when the founder of the band got to know *Punk Hardcore*. It's a really intense, abrasive and pulsating project that uses both traditional instruments, like electric guitars as well as samples, synths, tapes and distorted voices.

BAND MEMBERS
Al Jourgensen
Stephen George
Paul Barker

FORMED IN 1981

ORIGIN Chicago, IL

GENRE Industrial, Thrash Metal, Alternative Rock, Synth-pop

FAMOUS SONGS
Stigmata
Jesus Built My Hotrod
Burning Inside

In 1997 Time magazine considered Trent Reznor one of the 25 Most Influential Americans.

BAND MEMBERS
Trent Reznor
(only constant member)

FORMED IN 1988

ORIGIN Cleveland, OH

GENRE Alternative Rock, Industrial, Experimental

FAMOUS SONGS
Wish
The Perfect Drug
We're in This Together
Hurt

OTHER MUSICIANS
be all ears

THROBBING GRISTLE
Subhuman
United

FRONT 242
Headhunter
Tragedy For You

DIE KRUPPS
Bloodsuckers
To the Hilt

SKINNY PUPPY
Assimilate
Dig It

SWANS
New Mind
Just a Little Boy

KMFDM
UAIOE
A Drug Against War

THE YOUNG GODS
Gasoline Man
Kissing the Sun

FRONT LINE ASSEMBLY
Millennium
Neologic Spasm

FEAR FACTORY
Martyr
Replica

RAMMSTEIN
Heirate Mich
Du Hast

NINE INCH NAILS

Trent was born in a small town where he studied piano, sax, tuba and organ. He moved to Cleveland, where he played with some bands and worked as an assistant at a music studio; the ideal place for him to make his initial recordings. He could not find a band that understood his ideas and, inspired by Prince, he played all instruments except drums. Unlike the vast majority of *Industrial* artists, Trent wrote traditionally structured melodic songs, where lyrics are really important. His *Pop* instincts made the aggressive *Industrial* electronic rhythms easier on the ears, while also giving a human face to a style that seems entirely mechanical. Nine Inch Nails were the most popular *Industrial* band ever and they were responsible for delivering the genre to the masses.

MARILYN MANSON

Brian Warner is Marilyn Manson's real name. In 1989, he formed Marilyn Manson and the Spooky Kids, a band where each member's name was a combination of the first name of an icon of feminine sensuality and the surname of a serial killer. Taking inspiration from Alice Cooper, Ozzy Osbourne, David Bowie and horror books, Marilyn Manson became one of the most infamous and despised figures in '90s *Rock* history. Parents' associations and religious and political figures protested his music and live performances, which only made the band even more popular. Charismatic, sincere and provocative, Manson defended himself by saying that the most important thing was music and arts.

BAND MEMBERS
Marilyn Manson
(only constant member)

FORMED IN 1989

ORIGIN Fort Lauderdale, FL

GENRE Industrial, Alternative Rock, Glam Rock

FAMOUS SONGS
Tourniquet
The Beautiful People
I Don't Like the Drugs

Manson uses contact lenses with different pupil sizes on each eye as a tribute to David Bowie.

Grunge is a musical style that was born in Seattle, in the American Northwest, and became extremely popular during the first half of the '90s. It took off with the release of Nirvana's *Nevermind* and Pearl Jam's *Ten*. The success these bands had, as well as others like Soundgarden and Alice in Chains, made *Grunge* one of the most popular *Rock* forms of that era. Lyrics touch on angst, loneliness and a desire for freedom. *Grunge*'s visual style was uncomplicated, and many of its musicians had sloppy looks and rejected theatrics in their shows.

Kurt Cobain became the image of a generation. His sloppy looks, simple, baggy clothes, shaggy long hair and torn jeans were the exact opposite of '80s Rock elaborate styles.

NIRVANA

Kurt was born in the small city of Aberdeen, Washington. His parents got divorced when he was 8, forcing him to live with other family members and move from one household to another. He became an angst-ridden teen who would pour all his bitterness and rage into music. He became Nirvana's singer and guitar player, together with Krist Novoselic on bass and Dave Grohl (later the singer in Foo Fighters) on drums. The band hit it big with the release, in 1991, of their album *Nevermind*. Its first single, *Smells Like Teen Spirit*, was revolutionary. The initial chords of the song changed *Rock* history, shattering the eardrums of old people and making young ones jump around. Nirvana recorded only three album's worth of original material but became one of the most important and famous bands in the *Alternative Rock* world, and a huge influence in many young musicians through their raw, direct and straightforward music.

BAND MEMBERS
Kurt Cobain
Krist Novoselic
Chad Channing
Dave Grohl

FORMED IN 1987

ORIGIN Aberdeen, WA

GENRE Grunge, Alternative Rock

FAMOUS SONGS
About a Girl
Smells Like Teen Spirit
Come as You Are
Heart-Shaped Box

SOUNDGARDEN

Soundgarden was one of the first *Grunge* bands. In 1984, Chris, Kim and Hiro got together and formed the band. Chris originally played drums and sang, but in 1985 the band recruited Scott (who was quickly substituted by Matt) to let Chris focus on vocals. For the next two years the band played in Seattle and met Bruce Pavitt, the future founder of *Sub Pop*, the legendary Seattle record label that released their first EP, *Screaming Life*. Despite the fact they were *Grunge*'s oldest act, Soundgarden reached wide success later than others; they only became well-known in 1994 with the album *Superunknown*, and its single, *Black Hole Sun*. Their music was pretty heavy, mixing *Rock*, *Metal*, *Psychedelic* and *Punk Rock* with Chris Cornell's powerful voice hitting piercing highs and guttural lows.

The name Soundgarden comes from a sound sculpture located in a park in Seattle, their hometown.

BAND MEMBERS
Chris Cornell
Kim Thayil
Hiro Yamamoto
Matt Cameron
Ben Shepherd
Scott Sundquist

FORMED IN 1984

ORIGIN Seattle, WA

GENRE Grunge, Heavy Metal, Hard Rock, Alternative Rock

FAMOUS SONGS
Rusty Cage
Spoonman
Black Hole Sun
Fell on Black Days

They took the band name from a booster guitar effect pedal.

SCREAMING TREES

This quartet included the Conner brothers and two guys named Mark: Lanegan and Pickerel. It was Steve Fisk, a member of another band, who convinced a label to sign them and release their first album. At the beginning, Screaming Trees' music blended *Psychedelic Rock* and *Garage Rock*. This sound and Mark Lanegan's seductive, dark and anguished voice were the right elements to fit them into the movement that was on the verge of exploding: *Grunge*. The *Nevermind* phenomenon ended up helping all the bands around Nirvana, and Screaming Trees was one of them. In 1992 they saw their track *Nearly Lost You* added to the film *Singles* original soundtrack. The track became a hit but the band would never reach the success that their peers achieved. Mark Lanegan went on to a successful solo career.

BAND MEMBERS
Mark Lanegan
Gary Lee Conner
Van Conner
Mark Pickerel
Barrett Martin

FORMED IN 1985

ORIGIN Ellensburg, WA

GENRE Alternative Rock, Grunge, Psychedelic

FAMOUS SONGS
Nearly Lost You
Dollar Bill
Shadow of the Season
All I Know

L7

Suzi, Donita, Dee and Jennifer were associated with the *Grunge* movement due to their style, sound and attitude, but they were actually far away from Seattle. Just like many other bands, they became well-known for their live performances. Success arrived in 1992 with their *Bricks are Heavy* album. These four girls came to show the world that you don't have to be sexy or pretty to be onstage. In fact, the band tried to prove the opposite: they thought the audiences and critics should focus more on the music and less on the fact that this was a women-only band. Still, they had a unique style, with their large t-shirts, torn jeans and scruffy hair dyed blue, red or white (which is all the rage nowadays!).

🇺🇸

BAND MEMBERS
Donita Sparks
Suzi Gardner
Jennifer Finch
Dee Plakas

FORMED IN 1985

ORIGIN Los Angeles, CA

GENRE Grunge, Punk Rock, Alternative Rock, Heavy Metal

FAMOUS SONGS
Pretend We're Dead
Everglade
Monster

In the 1994 Lollapalooza Music Festival, Donita roller skated through the stage during Nick Cave's performance and bumped into the singer!

Alice in Chains loved Hard Rock and Heavy Metal and their music was heavily influenced by these genres.

ALICE IN CHAINS

Jerry and Layne were already playing in bands when they met at a party. They ended up becoming housemates and later bandmates, together with their friends Mike Starr and Sean Kinney. Their sound was a perfect fit for the *Alternative Rock* movement that was brewing in their corner of the USA. Yes, you guessed it: *Grunge*. Jerry's furious and melancholic guitar sound was the perfect backdrop for Layne's deep voice and tormented lyrics. The band rose to fame in 1992 with the release of the track *Would?*, and yet the band was in a bit of trouble, with Mike Starr leaving and being replaced by Mike Inez. With Layne's death in 2002 the band members dispersed, but later Jerry, Sean and Mike Inez regrouped with the arrival of singer William, and are still playing today. Older fans say it's not the same, though.

🇺🇸

BAND MEMBERS
Layne Staley
Mike Starr
Jerry Cantrell
Sean Kinney
Mike Inez
William DuVall

FORMED IN 1987

ORIGIN Seattle, WA

GENRE Grunge, Heavy Metal, Alternative Rock, Hard Rock

FAMOUS SONGS
Man in the Box
Would?
Down in a Hole
Rooster
No Excuses

Eddie Vedder was an incredible acrobat. Once he climbed the stage scaffolding and was responsible for the biggest stage dive ever.

Pearl Jam promote numerous causes like protection of wildlife or rejection of hate speech.

PEARL JAM

Green River came to be known as the first *Grunge* band. When they split, half of its members formed Mudhoney, while Stone and Jeff, future elements in Pearl Jam, joined Mother Love Bone, which for a short time was one of the *Grunge* sensations in Seattle but would soon break apart too. Stone and Jeff started to record demos with guitarist Mike while they were looking for a drummer and a singer. One such recording landed in the hands of a young Californian surfer, Eddie Vedder, who listened to the songs before grabbing his surfboard and creating the lyrics while surfing. He recorded his singing over the tape and sent it back, and Pearl Jam was formed. By 1992 they were already one of the most popular bands worldwide. Even though their sound was not as heavy as other *Grunge* bands, their musical intensity and Eddie's clenched teeth guaranteed them a bright future and a singular longevity. Pearl Jam are still one of today's most successful and hard-working groups in *Rock*.

BAND MEMBERS
Eddie Vedder
Mike McCready
Stone Gossard
Jeff Ament
Dave Krusen
Dave Abbruzzese
Matt Cameron

FORMED IN 1990

ORIGIN Seattle, WA

GENRE Alternative Rock, Grunge

FAMOUS SONGS
Alive
Jeremy
Oceans
Daughter
Do the Evolution
The Fixer

OTHER MUSICIANS
be all ears

MELVINS
Honey Bucket
Boris

GREEN RIVER
Together We'll Never
Swallow My Pride

MOTHER LOVE BONE
This Is Shangrila
Chloe Dancer

MUDHONEY
Good Enough
Touch Me I'm Sick

STONE TEMPLE PILOTS
Big Empty
Interstate Love Song

HOLE
Miss World
Celebrity Skin

TEMPLE OF THE DOG
Hunger Strike
Say Hello 2 Heaven

SILVERCHAIR
Tomorrow
Israel's Son

MAD SEASON
River of Deceit
Wake Up

In the final decade of the last millennium, *Rock* remained popular through its various offshoots. By that time, the main genres were *Grunge, Britpop, Industrial Rock, Pop Punk* and *Electronic*. The artists in this section have the '90s in common. Some, like Pavement and Morphine, peaked in it; others, like Beck and Foo Fighters, started to become successful in that decade and kept going through the next ones; others still started their promising careers in the '90s, like Muse or Queens of the Stone Age.

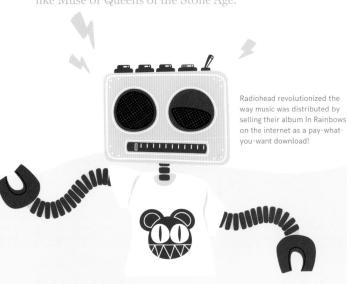

Radiohead revolutionized the way music was distributed by selling their album In Rainbows on the internet as a pay-what-you-want download!

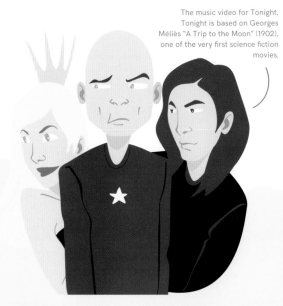

The music video for Tonight, Tonight is based on Georges Méliès "A Trip to the Moon" (1902), one of the very first science fiction movies.

RADIOHEAD

Thom Yorke was a shy and lonely kid. When he started his band he chose Ed for guitar because he reminded him of Morrissey and bass player Colin because of his flashy dress and outgoing personality. Later, Jonny got into the band too. Initially they went by the name On a Friday but, in 1992, they changed it to Radiohead, a Talking Heads song title. Their first album, *Pablo Honey*, included the single *Creep*, which became the band's biggest hit. The albums *OK Computer* and *Kid A* were considered musical revolutions where *Rock* tried to combine with *Electronic* in a poignant and melancholic but also beautiful way.

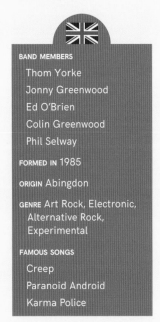

BAND MEMBERS
Thom Yorke
Jonny Greenwood
Ed O'Brien
Colin Greenwood
Phil Selway

FORMED IN 1985

ORIGIN Abingdon

GENRE Art Rock, Electronic, Alternative Rock, Experimental

FAMOUS SONGS
Creep
Paranoid Android
Karma Police

THE SMASHING PUMPKINS

Billy worked at a record store when he paired up with guitarist James. Inspired by The Cure, they formed Smashing Pumpkins. Later D'Arcy and Jimmy got in too, and together they explored heavier music territory. All their '90s albums were instant hits. By the time heavier music reigned, Smashing Pumpkins were adding more complex melodies, closer to *Prog Rock* than to *Grunge* or *Punk*. Their songs showed a harmony between musicians and their instrumental quality, and Billy's dense and dreamy lyrics, elevating the band to the upper level in *Alternative Rock*.

BAND MEMBERS
Billy Corgan
James Iha
D'arcy Wretzky
Jimmy Chamberlin

FORMED IN 1988

ORIGIN Chicago, IL

GENRE Alternative Rock

FAMOUS SONGS
Today
Bullet with Butterfly Wings
Tonight, Tonight

THE BREEDERS

While still a member of Pixies, Kim founded The Breeders with Tanya from Throwing Muses. Kelley, Kim's twin sister, only joined the band in 1992 and didn't even knew how to play the guitar at that time. Their most successful album, 1993's Last Splash, was made famous by a fun song called Cannonball.

BAND MEMBERS

Kim Deal; Tanya Donelly; Kelley Deal; Britt Walford; Jim MacPherson; Josephine Wiggs

FORMED IN 1989

ORIGIN Boston, MA

GENRE Alternative Rock

FAMOUS SONGS

Cannonball

Divine Hammer

Do You Love Me Now?

BAND MEMBERS

Stephen Malkmus; Scott Kannberg; Mark Ibold; Steve West; Bob Nastanovich

FORMED IN 1989

ORIGIN Stockton, CA

GENRE Alternative Rock, Lo-fi

FAMOUS SONGS

Cut Your Hair

Gold Soundz

Shady Lane

PAVEMENT

Stephen had finished studying history when he formed Pavement with Scott, his childhood friend. The band never wanted to be successful and yet their apparently un-tuned and confusing music, and Stephen's laid back voice, made them one of the most original Alternative Rock bands in the '90s. They became associated with another genre called Lo-fi.

MORPHINE

Nothing quite like it had been seen when Morphine hit the scene. A Rock band with no guitar? The trio played bass, drums and saxophone with a seductive voice on top of it, a Rock sound but tinted with Jazz and Blues. The singer played with a 2-string bass guitar and the sax player sometimes played with two saxes at the same time!

BAND MEMBERS

Mark Sandman; Dana Colley; Jerome Deupree; Billy Conway

FORMED IN 1989

ORIGIN Cambridge, MA

GENRE Alternative Rock, Jazz

FAMOUS SONGS

Buena

Cure for Pain

I'm Free Now

Honey White

BJÖRK

Björk Guðmundsdóttir (try to pronounce that!) was born in Reykjavik, Iceland, and studied piano and flute as a child. Her teachers were so impressed with her voice at a school recital that they sent out a recording of it to Iceland's national radio. Everyone in the country heard it and a label got interested in it and Björk got to release her first album by 12. During her adolescence, she went through some *Jazz*, *Punk* and *Goth Rock* bands until she finally joined Sugarcubes as their singer, achieving some success by the late '80s. During the next decade, she decided to move to London and pursue a solo career. Her visual style is quite eccentric and avant-garde and her voice is quite elastic, light and fragile while also robust. She deep-dived in *Pop* and *Electronic* music and became one of the biggest stars in the '90s.

DEBUT ALBUM 1992 (solo)

ORIGIN Reykjavik

GENRE Pop, Art Rock, Experimental, Electronic, Avant-garde

FAMOUS SONGS

Human Behaviour

Venus as a Boy

Big Time Sensuality

It's Oh So Quiet

Bjork is well known for her eccentric visual style; she has worn a dress in the shape of a swan, alien-like outfits and diamonds glued to her face.

Aged 16, Beck worked as a street musician.

BECK

Born Bek David Campbell, Beck came from a family of artists and spent his childhood between California and Kansas. After trying his luck in New York, he returned to LA where he was found by *Bong Load*'s label owner. He recorded some songs there, mixing *Hip-Hop* beats with samples and *Rock*. Out of these experiences the song *Loser*, his biggest hit, was born. Still, Beck didn't stop mixing genres and wanted to embrace all that music had to offer, drawing songs based on *Hip-Hop*, *Blues*, *Rock*, *Folk*, *Pop*, *Soul*, *Funk*, *Psychedelic* and *Electronic*, confirming that it is important to look at the past to build the future.

DEBUT ALBUM 1993

ORIGIN Los Angeles, CA

GENRE Alternative Rock, Pop, Folk, Electronic, Hip-Hop, Rap

FAMOUS SONGS

Loser

Where it's At

Devils Haircut

Heart is a Drum

PJ HARVEY

Polly Jean Harvey grew up on a farm and her parents got her into some *Rock*, *Folk* and *Blues* artists, Bob Dylan being the one she liked best. She belonged to a few *Folk* bands in her hometown and in 1988 she started playing guitar and saxophone with *Automatic Dlamini*. In 1991 she formed the PJ Harvey Trio with two members of her previous band, and they released two albums. The emotional power of their songs and the literary rawness of her lyrics gained them international success. Although she chose to go solo in 1993, PJ Harvey always looked for new artists to share experiences with. She's known for changing her looks with every new album, creating a unique look for herself, the record and the live shows.

PJ is also an actress and a sculptress. She plays several instruments like guitar, piano, vibraphone, marimba, bells, chimes, djembe, maracas, acordeon, autoharp, sitar, melodica, harp and cigar box guitar.

DEBUT ALBUM 1992

ORIGIN Bridport

GENRE Alternative Rock, Punk, Folk, Art Rock

FAMOUS SONGS
Down By the Water
Good Fortune
This Is Love
The Community of Hope

In 1995 he was nominated one of the 50 most beautiful people in the world. Jeff hated that!

David Bowie said "Grace" was the record he would take to a desert island.

JEFF BUCKLEY

Jeff was the son of Tim Buckley, a famous *Folk* and *Rock* artist. He lived many years under the shadow of his father; he was compared to him, despite having been in his presence only once, when he was 8. His stepdad was actually a lot closer to Jeff and he was the one who inspired him to follow his passion for music. He played in several bands until he went solo in 1992. The *Sin-é* (pronounced shih-NAY) became his weekly stage, drawing in more and more fans. His taste was all over the place: he could sing Édith Piaf one night and The Smiths the next. His beautiful voice and the sensitivity and intensity with which he sang attracted a label who would soon launch his first and only album, one that is still being discovered by new fans.

DEBUT ALBUM 1992

ORIGIN Orange, CA

GENRE Alternative Rock, Folk Rock, Soul, Blues

FAMOUS SONGS
Grace
Last Goodbye
So Real
Hallelujah (popularized by)

Matt Bellamy holds the Guinness record for highest number of guitars destroyed in a tour: 140.

Did you know that Matt Bellamy used his zipper as a music instrument?

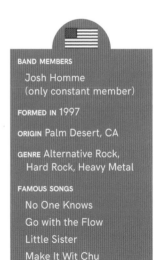

Beyond Queens of the Stone Age, Josh Homme participated in projects like Kyuss, Eagles of Death Metal and Them Crooked Vultures; he also collaborated with Iggy Pop.

MUSE

Just like Jeff Buckley, Matt Bellamy had a famous dad – George Bellamy, singer and guitar player for the British *Rock* band The Tornados. As a child, Matt dreamt of being a classical pianist, but changed his mind after attending a Rage Against the Machine concert. He joined his friends Chris and Dominic and formed Rocket Baby Dolls. They decided to participate in a battle of the bands contest just for fun, but ended up winning it. They then changed their name to Muse. The band took almost a decade to reach wide success but they got there with their third album, *Absolution*; from there on it was a piece of cake.

Their *Prog Rock* style and electronic exploration earn them the sale of millions of records and sold out stadiums throughout the world.

BAND MEMBERS
Matt Bellamy
Chris Wolstenholme
Dominic Howard

FORMED IN 1994

ORIGIN Teignmouth

GENRE Alternative Rock, Progressive Rock, Hard Rock, Electronic

FAMOUS SONGS
Knights of Cydonia
Uprising
Hysteria
Time Is Running Out
Plug In Baby

QUEENS OF THE STONE AGE

Queens of the Stone Age (QOTSA) were born out of the ashes of a band called Kyuss. Many musicians came and went, but QOTSA always had a permanent member: Josh Homme. In 1995 Josh left Kyuss and played for a year with the *Grunge* band Screaming Trees (Page 77), yet he did not identify with that sound and decided to create a project that would satisfy him. Josh started to work with a group of musicians from different bands and, by 1998, he recorded QOTSA's first album. Since then and up until their latest work, countless talented musicians have

helped the band produce a very special kind of *Rock* (*Stoner Rock*) with hints of *Blues*, *Hard Rock* and *Heavy Metal*.

BAND MEMBERS
Josh Homme
(only constant member)

FORMED IN 1997

ORIGIN Palm Desert, CA

GENRE Alternative Rock, Hard Rock, Heavy Metal

FAMOUS SONGS
No One Knows
Go with the Flow
Little Sister
Make It Wit Chu

The term "Foo Fighters" is related to the UFO phenomena that were seen in the skies during World War II.

FOO FIGHTERS

After Nirvana disbanded, Dave, the drummer, picked up a guitar and formed Foo Fighters. Before Nirvana existed, he had already played in several bands and written his own songs, which he kept in a drawer from his teen years. Dave played all the instruments on Foo Fighters' first record and only then did he search for musicians for the tour: bassist Nate, drummer William and guitarist Pat. The following album became a huge success, especially due to the hit singles *My Hero* and *Everlong*. Still, they could hardly guess they would be one of the few bands to survive the *Alternative Rock* explosion from the '90s and even less that they would become one of the biggest *Rock* bands in the world, filling out stadiums and selling millions of records. Yet that was how it went and they released hit after hit, combining heavy guitars, *Punk* sensibility (although less and less as time went by) and *Pop* melodies, getting the *Rock* formula right. Dave Grohl is a very busy man; when he is not playing with Foo Fighters he collaborates with other musicians like Paul McCartney, Garbage, Nine Inch Nails, David Bowie, The Prodigy, Slash, Iggy Pop, Tom Petty, Lemmy, Stevie Nicks and many more.

BAND MEMBERS
Dave Grohl
Franz Stahl
William Goldsmith
Nate Mendel
Taylor Hawkins
Pat Smear
Chris Shiflett

FORMED IN 1994

ORIGIN Seattle, WA

GENRE Alternative Rock, Hard Rock

FAMOUS SONGS
Big Me
Monkey Wrench
Everlong
My Hero
Learn to Fly
Times Like These
The Pretender

AS BRIT AS IT GETS

The bands that appear on these pages share the same genre, *Britpop*, a style that came out of the UK in the '90s. This cultural movement was seen as a reaction to heavier North-American music, like *Grunge*. These musicians got their inspiration from the British musical roots of prior decades to create a guitar-driven melodic blend of *Pop* and *Rock* which brought forth freshness and lightness in their music and lyrics.

Damon Albarn created the band Gorillaz. They released six albums but the musicians never showed themselves rather appearing as cartoons.

In 1994 Liam hit Noel with a tambourine, on stage, which made the guitarist temporarily leave the band.

BLUR

Damon, Graham, Alex and Dave got together in 1989 and created Seymour. After some concerts and a demo, the label Food got interested in the band and invited them to record their first album, *Leisure*, under their new moniker, Blur. At the beginning they were influenced a bit by the Manchester sound, especially by Stone Roses, but throughout their career they fine-tuned their style and created *Pop* melodies infused with *Rock* energy. Their 90s records were hugely successful, carrying them to the *Britpop* throne, always in a tight competition with Oasis. The exuberant "woo-hoo" on *Song 2* became a true hymn. By the end of the decade they got tired of such rivalries and drew away from *Britpop*, surprising fans with each new innovative album.

BAND MEMBERS
Damon Albarn
Graham Coxon
Alex James
Dave Rowntree

FORMED IN 1989

ORIGIN London

GENRE Alternative Rock, Britpop

FAMOUS SONGS
Girls & Boys
Parklife
Country House
The Universal
Song 2

OASIS

The Gallagher brothers come from Manchester. Noel, who was a roadie for Inspiral Carpets, arrived home one day to see that his brother Liam had formed a band, and he was invited to join. He accepted on the condition of being its leader. The truth is that Noel had some well-defined ideas on music and a few songs already written. Some people say Oasis are not very original, drawing perhaps too much from previous English bands (The Rolling Stones' posture, The Beatles' melodies, Sex Pistols' rebelliousness and Stone Roses' arrogance) but the fact of the matter is that they've created some very powerful and beautiful songs, and there was once a time in which they ruled *Britpop*, outperforming Blur (at least in record sales). Still, Blur carried on and Oasis didn't.

BAND MEMBERS
Liam Gallagher
Paul "Bonehead" Arthurs
Paul "Guigsy" McGuigan
Tony McCarroll
Noel Gallagher

FORMED IN 1991

ORIGIN Manchester

GENRE Rock, Britpop

FAMOUS SONGS
Roll with It
Wonderwall
Don't Look Back in Anger
Champagne Supernova

Jarvis Cocker was once trying to impress a girl and fell 32 feet to the pavement and broke several bones. Even on a wheelchair, he kept on playing live!

Comedian Ricky Gervais was once Suede's manager.

PULP

A lot of bands achieve overnight success and then fade away; others slowly rise up to the top. Pulp's case was neither. Pulp was started as a college project by singer Jarvis Cocker in 1978. They played and released records that almost no one heard. After many changes in their line-up (more than 20 musicians came and went), visual style and sound (they went through *Post-Punk*, *Glam Rock*, *Disco*, *New Wave* and *House*), by the mid-90s they settled on *Britpop*, achieving considerable success 15 years after they started. Their danceable melodies and Jarvis's funny lyrics contributed to their success. Here's a challenge: try to listen to the song *Common People* without jumping up and down!

BAND MEMBERS
Jarvis Cocker
Candida Doyle
Russell Senior
Mark Webber
Steve Mackey
Nick Banks

FORMED IN 1978

ORIGIN Sheffield

GENRE Britpop, Art Rock

FAMOUS SONGS
Babies
Do You Remember the First Time?
Common People
Disco 2000

SUEDE

In 1992, British music magazine *Melody Maker* presented Suede as the best new band in the United Kingdom. That came as a bit of a surprise because the band hadn't yet released a record. This popularity can be explained by their electrifying concerts, which were spread through word of mouth throughout the city and the country. Suede, being fans of David Bowie and The Smiths, reinvented *Glam Rock* in a refreshing way, making it more *Pop*. They mixed the decadent elegance of *Glam* with the tortured angst of British *Post-Punk*. This type of music was seen as a way to compensate for the more aggressive sound that was heard then, mainly *Grunge* and some of the *Alternative Rock* that was being released at the time.

BAND MEMBERS
Brett Anderson
Bernard Butler
Mat Osman
Simon Gilbert
Richard Oakes
Neil Codling

FORMED IN 1989

ORIGIN London

GENRE Alternative Rock, Britpop, Glam Rock

FAMOUS SONGS
So Young
Trash
Beautiful Ones
She's in Fashion

On the left page of this section you'll find two of the most important *Trip Hop* bands: Massive Attack, genre creators, and Portishead, who became well-known in their genre. They're both from Bristol; the cradle for this music that blends *Hip-Hop*, *Dub* and *Electronic* and uses a lot of samples and hypnotic voices. The bands to the right have a stronger beat and their (main) genre is *Big Beat* – you could say it is electronic music with really strong and energetic beats mixed with samples and vocals. *Rock* guitars and their spirit are present in all of these bands. The best representatives of the genre are The Chemical Brothers, who created it, and The Prodigy, who made it faster and took it further, proving that an electronic band can satisfy even the most demanding *Rock* fans.

No one knows the true identity of Banksy, the world's best known street artist, but a lot of people suspect it could be Robert Del Naja.

Portishead don't really like to give interviews.

MASSIVE ATTACK

It all started in Bristol, when a group of DJs, rappers, singers and producers called Wild Bunch started to organize street parties where they combined *Hip-Hop* and samples, smartly cued by the DJs, with *Soul* melodies wrapped in *Reggae* and *Dub* sounds. In 1987, two members of this collective of artists, Andrew and Grant, joined Robert, a talented graffiti artist, and they formed Massive Attack. The group found their own sound within this remixing spirit: dark and melancholic rhythms, echo-drenched guitars, rich samples and steady beats that helped create the blueprint for what *Trip Hop* came to be. Their initial records became all-time classics not just for the fans of the genre but for audiences in general.

BAND MEMBERS
Robert Del Naja
Grant Marshall
Andrew Vowles

FORMED IN 1987

ORIGIN Bristol

GENRE Trip Hop, Electronic, Alternative Rock

FAMOUS SONGS
Unfinished Sympathy
Safe from Harm
Protection
Teardrop

PORTISHEAD

Portishead didn't invent *Trip Hop* but were the ones that helped take it further and made it more interesting for the *Alternative Rock* crowd. Beth and Geoff met in Bristol's Job Centre at a time where both were unemployed, and they found out that they had so much in common that they decided to unite musically, with a helping hand from guitar player Adrian and sound engineer Dave. Beth had an angelic voice and Geoff had already produced songs for several artists. Inspired by Massive Attack beats, Portishead added elements of *Jazz* and *House* and samples from old espionage movies, creating a magical, hypnotic and somewhat dark result.

BAND MEMBERS
Geoff Barrow
Beth Gibbons
Adrian Utley

FORMED IN 1991

ORIGIN Bristol

GENRE Trip Hop, Electronic, Alternative Rock

FAMOUS SONGS
Sour Times
Glory Box
Roads
It's a Fire

THE CHEMICAL BROTHERS

Tom and Edward met in college at the end of the '80s. They were both into *House*, *Techno* and *Hip-Hop* and started DJing at parties using Dust Brothers as their artistic name, as a tribute to two *Hip-Hop* producers. Their act was so successful they were soon invited to spin records at a club and create their own songs. By the '90s they had to change their name to The Chemical Brothers to avoid confusion with the original Dust Brothers. In 1995 they launched *Exit Planet Dust* and, two years later, their most successful album, *Dig Your Own Hole*, made them the pioneers of a new sub-genre within electronic dance music that came to be known as *Big Beat*.

BAND MEMBERS
Tom Rowlands
Edward Simonsy

FORMED IN 1989

ORIGIN Manchester

GENRE Big Beat, Electronic, Techno, Trip Hop, House

FAMOUS SONGS
Setting Sun
Where Do I Begin
Block Rockin' Beats
Hey Boy Hey Girl

Oasis singer Liam Gallagher picked a fight with the Chemical Brothers because he did not like the songs they chose for a DJ set at the end of his concert.

THE PRODIGY

Prodigy have a very unique visual style: Keith dyed and shaved his hair and Maxim used cat eye contact lenses.

Despite having classical piano training, Liam enjoyed *Hip-Hop* and *House*. He soon became a DJ and started recording music in his room. By 1990, his path crossed those of Keith, Maxim and Leeroy at a club in Essex, and they decided to form The Prodigy. Keith's and Leeroy's intention was to dance, giving strength to the music and creating a wild party ambience. The band released their first album in 1992 and, two years later, the lauded *Music for the Jilted Generation*. In 1997 the band "exploded" worldwide with the launch of the highly successful *The Fat of the Land*. Their mixture of electronic music (*Big Beat*), *Punk* and *Rock* was responsible for the union of tribes until then separated by a sea of prejudice.

BAND MEMBERS
Liam Howlett
Keith Flint
Maxim
Leeroy Thornhill
Sharky

FORMED IN 1990

ORIGIN Braintree

GENRE Techno, Rock, Punk, Electronic, Big Beat

FAMOUS SONGS
No Good
Voodoo People
Poison
Firestarter
Breathe

OTHER MUSICIANS
be all ears

FATBOY SLIM
The Rockafeller Skank
Praise You
Right Here, Right Now

UNDERWORLD
Underneath the Radar
Cowgirl
Born Slippy

TRICKY
Aftermath
Overcome
Ponderosa

PROPELLERHEADS
Take California
History Repeating
Bang On

GROOVE ARMADA
I See You Baby
Superstylin'
My Friend

LCD SOUNDSYSTEM
Daft Punk is Playing at My House
North American Scum
All My Friends

Bands on these pages were created in yet another music melting pot, combining *Heavy Metal* with *Rap* in different ways. In the first two pages, there's Rage Against the Machine, who together with Body Count are prime examples of *Rap Metal*. They were inspired by other bands that fused *Rock* and *Hip-Hop* (page 68) but added extra heaviness. In the last two pages, you'll see *Nu Metal* bands; this is a similar genre but with thinner voices. At the dawn of the new millennium this genre became very popular through bands like Korn, System of a Down, Linkin Park and Limp Bizkit.

They used a famous picture of the South-American guerilla fighter Che Guevara, which led many to think he was the singer.

RAGE AGAINST THE MACHINE

Zack and Tom were raised in activist families and were influenced by the values of their parents. In California, Tom met Zack and soon understood that, just like him, he had a rebellious and political spirit. With drummer Brad and bassist Tim they formed Rage Against the Machine in 1991. Inspired by the powerful instruments in *Metal* and the voices and rhythms of *Rap*, they developed a unique style with Zack's powerful rhymes and furious energy and with Tom's amazing guitar technique. In 1992 they released their explosive first album, which included a track that talks about corruption and racism in America's police force: *Killing in the Name*. It included a clear rejection: "I won't do what you tell me!" Young people who listened to it identified with the controversial lyrics while jumping up and down to the furious beat.

BAND MEMBERS
Zack de la Rocha
Tom Morello
Tim Commerford
Brad Wilk

FORMED IN 1991

ORIGIN Los Angeles, CA

GENRE Rap Metal, Funk, Alternative Rock

FAMOUS SONGS
Killing in the Name
Bullet in the Head
Bulls on Parade

Ice-T wrote a lot of songs criticizing the police but he plays a police inspector in a very famous TV series, Law & Order: Special Victims Unit.

BODY COUNT

Tracy Marrow, better known as Ice-T, lost his parents when he was a child and ended up in an orphanage. Then he went to live with an aunt in Los Angeles. Tracy lived through most of his adolescence and young adult years angry at the racism that he felt daily. Until the time music saved him Tracy was no choirboy, far from it! There were a lot of gangs in his neighborhood and it was hard to stay away from them. Despite his many offenses as a young man, Tracy liked to read and listen to music. He used to bust some rhymes for his buddies and was a DJ for a while. He started his rapper career as a solo act, Ice-T. When he recorded his fourth album he decided to mix *Rap* with *Heavy Metal* in one of its songs, just for fun. The song is titled *Body Count* and that became the name of a band. He liked the result and so did his fans. Body Count got bigger and infamous due to their lyrics against police violence and racism. Ice-T defended himself by saying that these were just songs that expressed their life experiences. The band is still one of the most important *Rap Metal* acts, despite having only two of the original members.

BAND MEMBERS
Ice-T
Ernie C.
Mooseman
D-Roc
Beatmaster "V"

FORMED IN 1990

ORIGIN Los Angeles, CA

GENRE Thrash Metal, Hardcore Punk, Rap Metal

FAMOUS SONGS
There Goes the Neighborhood
Body Count's in the House
Born Dead

OTHER MUSICIANS
be all ears

CLAWFINGER
Do What I Say
Biggest & the Best

DEFTONES
My Own Summer
Change

TOOL
Sober
Ænema

P.O.D.
Alive
Youth of the Nation

PAPA ROACH
Last Resort
Between Angels And Insects

STAIND
It's Been Awhile
Fade

SLIPKNOT
Duality
Psychosocial

Korn were the first band to perform an interactive radio transmission through the internet.

KORN

The band had its origins in a *Metal* band named LAPD which consisted of guitarists James and Brian, bass player Reginald and drummer David. Their path crossed Jonathan's; a young man who wanted to be a mortician but who was also a singer in a band. Jonathan joined the band, and they named it Korn. Their two initial albums were successful but in 1998 they became world famous with *Follow the Leader*, even reaching #1 in the American charts. Korn have become known as the pioneers of *Nu Metal* with the dawn of the new millennium, paving the way for bands like Limp Bizkit, Deftones and Linkin Park.

BAND MEMBERS
James Shaffer
Reginald Arvizu
Brian Welch
Jonathan Davis
David Silveria

FORMED IN 1992

ORIGIN Bakersfield, CA

GENRE Nu Metal

FAMOUS SONGS
Got The Life
Freak on a Leash

LIMP BIZKIT

Fred, Sam, John and Wes joined in 1994 to form a band that would mix *Rap* and *Rock*. Limp Bizkit played in their hometown bars and started gathering a following. They got noticed because of their provocative energy on stage but also due to the bizarre clothes their guitarist used; he seemed to be a member of Kiss! Their friendship with *Hip-Hop* group House of Pain led them to recruit a new element: DJ Lethal, in charge of the turntables. Limp Biskit's first album came out in 1997 and its initial success was boosted by another band, Korn, who helped them out by spreading the word, promoting their concerts and TV presentations. The next two albums would have enormous success, but the band started to decline after that. They were never really appreciated by music critics, but their legion of fans surely disagrees!

Guitarist Wes and his wife founded a cat rescue organization called "Motor Kitty Rescue."

BAND MEMBERS
Fred Durst
Sam Rivers
John Otto
DJ Lethal
Wes Borland

FORMED IN 1994

ORIGIN Jacksonville, FL

GENRE Nu Metal

FAMOUS SONGS
Break Stuff
Rollin'
Nookie

SYSTEM OF A DOWN

Singer Serj, guitar player Daron, bassist Shavo and drummer Andy were already playing together in a previous band called Soil, in 1993. In 1997, Andy injured his hand while practising martial arts, and they invited a new member – John – to the band. Two years after that, they started playing and – inspired by a poem written by Daron called *Victims of a Down* – the group decided to call themselves System of a Down. Their concerts were explosive and word soon spread out. In 1998 they released their first album and three years later *Toxicity*, which mixed several sub-genres of *Metal* and made them champions of the heavyweight class of that time – *Nu Metal*.

All band members are of Armenian-American origin. Three of them have a clear fascination with growing their goatees in unusual ways!

BAND MEMBERS
Serj Tankian
Daron Malakian
Shavo Odadjian
Andy Khachaturian
John Dolmayan

FORMED IN 1994

ORIGIN Glendale, CA

GENRE Nu Metal

FAMOUS SONGS
Chop Suey!
B.Y.O.B.
Toxicity

LINKIN PARK

Mike, Rob and Brad were high school colleagues and they used to play together. They recruited Mark, Dave and Joe to form a band called Xero. During the second half of the 1990s, they played and sent demos to record labels but had very little success. Frustrated with this, Mark decided to leave the band. Before the new millennium arrived, they found their new singer, Chester. They've changed their name to Linkin Park and were finally ready to launch their first album, *Hybrid Theory*. It became a massive global hit, selling more than 30 million copies. Unlike many other bands in this genre, Linkin Park's lyrics don't include lots of swearing; this, together with some melodic songs, helped them top the charts. After Chester's passing the band didn't break apart, but struggled to move forward without their leader.

Linkin Park were the first Rock band to achieve over one billion hits on YouTube.

BAND MEMBERS
Mike Shinoda
Rob Bourdon
Brad Delson
Mark Wakefield
Dave Farrell
Joe Hahn
Chester Bennington

FORMED IN 1996

ORIGIN Agoura Hills, CA

GENRE Nu Metal, Electronic

FAMOUS SONGS
In the End
Numb
Crawling

The 2000s didn't bring a lot of entirely new or even different music genres. *Alternative Rock* continued to dominate, creating a lot of bands that fused genres and played some fresh, new *Rock*. Some of the stars that we present in this section were inspired by *New Wave*, *Post-Punk* and *Garage Rock*. In this category there's also room for Amy Winehouse, a diva who did not sing *Rock* but who had a rebellious spirit. The biggest news that the millennium brought wasn't the type of music but the way we started to listen to it, through the internet. New video-sharing websites like YouTube, and apps like iTunes and later Spotify changed the way music reaches its fans.

THE WHITE STRIPES

Meg White was working in a bar when she met a young upholsterer called John Gillis. They fell in love, got married and started making music together. John adopted the name Jack White and in 1997 they performed their first show as The White Stripes. The marriage didn't last long but the music did. Becoming noticed at the turn of the millennium, their first two albums had original songs and

For a long time Jack and Meg told everyone they were siblings.

In 2003 Jack White landed #17 on Rolling Stone magazine's list of the 100 greatest guitarists.

Jack White continues to have a brilliant solo career and has even had time to form several bands.

Blues, *Folk* and *Rock* covers. By their third album, The White Stripes were already acclaimed for the refreshing simplicity they brought to *Rock*. After releasing *Elephant* in 2003, the band exploded and appeared everywhere: magazine covers, celebrity news and greatest albums lists. They became the most influential band of the decade thanks to their mix of *Blues* with abrasive and vibrant *Punk Rock*. You can hear crowds chanting their most famous song, *Seven Nation Army*, on many occasions, such as football games.

BAND MEMBERS
Jack White
Meg White

FORMED IN 1997

ORIGIN Detroit, MI

GENRE Blues, Rock, Garage, Punk

FAMOUS SONGS
Hotel Yorba
Fell in Love with a Girl
Seven Nation Army

THE STROKES

Aged 14, Julian started writing songs inspired by Nirvana. He met his future bandmates in his school years and they rehearsed after classes. In early 2000, the five friends got together in New York and started a new era for Alternative Rock. The single Last Nite was the spark that The Strokes used to blast through the radio and dance floors. Their first album, Is This It, earned them huge success and appraisal by the critics. It was fresh and energetic Rock for a good start to the millennium.

BAND MEMBERS
Julian Casablancas
Nick Valensi
Albert Hammond Jr.
Nikolai Fraiture
Fabrizio Moretti

FORMED IN 1998

ORIGIN New York, NY

GENRE Alternative Rock, Garage Rock, Post-Punk

FAMOUS SONGS
Last Nite
Someday
You Only Live Once

BAND MEMBERS
Matt Berninger
Aaron Dessner
Bryce Dessner
Bryan Devendorf
Scott Devendorf

FORMED IN 1999

ORIGIN Cincinnati, OH

GENRE Alternative Rock, Post-Punk

FAMOUS SONGS
Mistaken for Strangers
Mr. November
Fake Empire

THE NATIONAL

The National includes singer Matt and two sets of brothers. When they launched their first record, in 2001, they didn't consider themselves a "real" band and kept their day jobs. By 2005 they were able to start playing full-time thanks to the success of their album Alligator, followed by even more success with 2007's Boxer. Slowly, yet surely, their dark and elegant Rock kept bringing them more and more fans.

YEAH YEAH YEAHS

Yeah Yeah Yeahs also appeared at the turn of the millennium, with the ferocious Karen O helming their explosive Punk and Art Rock. Karen liked to dress in torn outfits, throw drinks at the audience and smash pineapples on her head. The sonic commotion of their initial albums winded down and the band focused on playing an ever more danceable Rock with some room left for intense ballads, like the track Maps.

BAND MEMBERS
Karen O
Nick Zinner
Brian Chase

FORMED IN 2000

ORIGIN New York, NY

GENRE Alternative Rock, Garage Rock, Post-Punk

FAMOUS SONGS
Miles Away
Maps
Heads Will Roll

COLDPLAY

BAND MEMBERS

Chris Martin

Guy Berryman

Jonny Buckland

Will Champion

FORMED IN 1998

ORIGIN London

GENRE Alternative Rock, Pop

FAMOUS SONGS

Yellow

Speed of Sound

Clocks

When Coldplay's first single, Yellow, started to play non-stop on the radio, nobody would have dreamed they would become one of the biggest bands of the new millennium, yet that was exactly what happened. The band's sound – elegant, melodic and a bit dramatic – coupled with Chris Martin's sentimental lyrics convinced audiences, and they became commercially successful. With every new album they have earned numerous music prizes and sold millions of records.

GOSSIP

Brace, Kathy and Beth got together to make music because they were bored; they said their town Searcy had nothing to do, and so decided to make everyone dance. They moved to Olympia and created Gossip. Beth Ditto's powerful diva voice and presence took them through an original path, starting with Rock and Blues and moving further into Pop and Disco but always with a Punk energy and attitude added to their dance floor beats.

BAND MEMBERS

Beth Ditto

Brace Paine

Kathy Mendonça

Hannah Blilie

FORMED IN 1999

ORIGIN Olympia, WA

GENRE Garage Rock, Punk, Alternative Rock, Pop

FAMOUS SONGS

Standing In The Way Of Control

Listen Up!

Heavy Cross

THE KILLERS

BAND MEMBERS

Brandon Flowers

Dave Keuning

Mark Stoermer

Ronnie Vannucci Jr.

FORMED IN 2001

ORIGIN Las Vegas, NV

GENRE Alternative Rock, Pop

FAMOUS SONGS

Mr. Brightside

Somebody Told Me

Human

Brandon Flowers, the band's singer, belongs to the Mormon religion (which has very strict rules), yet that didn't stop him from having a band. Brandon, David, Mark and Ronnie got together in 2002, two years before the release of their debut album Hot Fuss that made the band really popular. The Killers' danceable Rock pays tribute to the great '80s heroes of New Wave and Synth-pop, but it's perfectly adapted to the trends of the new millennium.

They were compared a lot to The White Stripes (and not always as a compliment, as the word on the street was they were a bad copy) because they are a guitar + drums duo and have a similar name. Jack White hates The Black Keys because he thinks they copied his style.

THE BLACK KEYS

Dan and Patrick knew each from childhood, but only saw each other again at the turn of the millennium when Dan realized he could not book concerts without a demo that would showcase his music. This is where his buddy Patrick comes in, as he had a home studio and decided to help him (which was great because they ended up forming a duo, The Black Keys, recording their first album in Patrick's basement). Even though they were appreciated for their hard and soulful *Blues* and *Rock*, they had to wait until their fifth album to become successful – and oh boy, successful they be-

came! With their *Brothers* and *El Camino* albums they sold millions of copies and even won *Grammys*.

BAND MEMBERS
Dan Auerbach
Patrick Carney

FORMED IN 2001

ORIGIN Akron, OH

GENRE Garage Rock, Blues Rock, Alternative Rock

FAMOUS SONGS
I'll Be Your Man
Tighten Up
Lonely Boy
Gold on the Ceiling
Little Black Submarines

They were one of the first bands to gather a lot of success through file sharing on the internet by the fans, which led to a label contract.

ARCTIC MONKEYS

It all started in 2002 when some friends – and future bandmates – got guitars for Christmas. The following summer they started to rehearse and, in 2003, started to play live and offer demos on CD to their fans. They didn't record that many CDs so fans made copies and spread out the band's music without them knowing. A fan created a profile for them on MySpace and they

became viral. Arctic Monkeys were really surprised to see audiences singing along without them having released an album. Their popularity landed them a contract with a label, releasing their first album in 2006. Their *Punk* energy and *Pop* melody, together with their amusing lyrics and Alex's accent, made them one of the most respected bands of the new millennium.

BAND MEMBERS
Alex Turner
Matt Helders
Jamie Cook
Nick O'Malley
Andy Nicholson

FORMED IN 2002

ORIGIN Sheffield

GENRE Alternative Rock, Pop, Garage Rock

FAMOUS SONGS
I Bet You Look Good (...)
Cornerstone
Do I Wanna Know?

AMY WINEHOUSE

Amy was always a rebellious kid; at 16 she was expelled from her drama class for lack of commitment and for having pierced her nose. That same year, a friend send a demo of songs Amy performed to a label. She was hired on the spot and at 20 she recorded her first album, which was praised for her fantastic voice and its original mixture of *Jazz, Pop, Soul* and *R&B*. The end of a relationship had a huge impact on Amy. She lost a lot of weight, covered herself with tattoos and wore a beehive hairstyle, which became her trademark. In her album *Back to Black* she channelled all of her suffering into music, writing beautifully sad songs that revealed her bittersweet voice. Amy sold millions of records and won countless prizes, yet her life ended too soon. Her songs will continue to touch her fans profoundly.

DEBUT ALBUM 2003

ORIGIN London

GENRE Soul, R&B, Jazz

FAMOUS SONGS

Rehab

You Know I'm No Good

Back to Black

Love Is a Losing Game

She couldn't stop singing, madly in love as she was with music. She loved Frank Sinatra and borrowed his name for the title of her first album.

ALABAMA SHAKES

Brittany started playing the guitar and writing songs when she was around 13 years old. Then she met Zac who, just like her, had a love for music, and they started playing together. Soon Steve joined on drums and Heath on the guitar. Alabama Shakes (initially simply Shakes) had their first hit through the internet: a blogger released one of their songs and it became a success, which in turn made labels search for them. Their mix-

Before the band became successful, Brittany worked in the post office and as a chef.

BAND MEMBERS

Brittany Howard

Zac Cockrell

Heath Fogg

Steve Johnson

FORMED IN 2009

ORIGIN Athens, AL

GENRE Blues, Rock, Soul

FAMOUS SONGS

Hold On

You Ain't Alone

Don't Wanna Fight

ture of *Blues, Rock* and *Soul* is especially powerful thanks to Brittany's profound and powerful voice.

Funeral got its title due to the deaths of relatives of several band members during the recording of the album, which brought a melancholy that can be sensed in some of its songs.

OTHER MUSICIANS
be all ears

THE HIVES
Hate to Say I Told You So
Tick Tick Boom

INTERPOL
Obstacle 1
C'mere

**BLACK REBEL
MOTORCYCLE CLUB**
Love Burns
Stop

THE KILLS
Future Stars Slow
Black Balloon

EAGLES OF DEATH METAL
I Only Want You
Wannabe in LA

THE LIBERTINES
Time For Heroes
Can't Stand Me Now

KINGS OF LEON
Molly's Chambers
Use Somebody

BLOC PARTY
Banquet
Helicopter

TV ON THE RADIO
Wolf Like Me
Province

FRANZ FERDINAND
Take Me Out
This Fire

KURT VILE
Wakin on a Pretty Day
Pretty Pimpin

FLORENCE AND THE MACHINE
Dog Days Are Over
Shake It Out

A PLACE TO BURY STRANGERS
To Fix the Gash in Your Head
I Know I'll See You

THEE OH SEES
Toe Cutter-Thumb Buster
The Dream

TY SEGALL
Girlfriend
Love Fuzz

COURTNEY BARNETT
Pedestrian at Best
Nobody Really Cares (...)

CAR SEAT HEADREST
Fill in the Blank
Drunk Drivers / Killer Whales

ROYAL BLOOD
Figure it Out
Little Monster

ARCADE FIRE

Legend says that Win saw Régine singing *Jazz* standards at an art exhibit and was charmed with her voice. They became partners, musically and personally. Soon the duo expanded and Richard, William (Win's brother), Tim, Jeremy and Howard joined. Most of these musicians play more than one instrument on stage, which contributes to the band's unique sound. Their concerts are pretty frenzied, not just because of their music but also because of the way they play: once in a concert in Portugal one of the members played the drums by hitting his drumsticks on the other guy's helmet! Their two initial albums, *Funeral* and *Neon Bible,* were considered as some of the best of the '00s. Album after album, the band piled up hits. They have been able to play with many of their idols, like David Bowie, Neil Young, Mick Jagger and Bruce Springsteen. For a lot of music lovers, Arcade Fire was the band that was missing in this new music landscape.

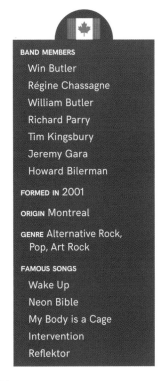

BAND MEMBERS
Win Butler
Régine Chassagne
William Butler
Richard Parry
Tim Kingsbury
Jeremy Gara
Howard Bilerman

FORMED IN 2001

ORIGIN Montreal

GENRE Alternative Rock,
Pop, Art Rock

FAMOUS SONGS
Wake Up
Neon Bible
My Body is a Cage
Intervention
Reflektor

As we've mentioned before, the bands that appeared at the turn of the millennium liked to mix many different genres. One of the most popular combinations was *Indie Folk* (which goes back to the early '90s), inspired by traditional *Folk* but also by *Alternative Rock*, which means they could probably enjoy both Neil Young and Radiohead. These bands use acoustic, traditional instruments but still combine them with electronic elements. Songs are quite melodic, lyrics are deep and the vocal harmonies bring to mind those of The Beach Boys (as in the case with Fleet Foxes) but with some effects-filled electronic touches (as with Grizzly Bear and Bon Iver).

Ed Droste is a fully dedicated musician; he's the one answering messages from fans.

They were originally called The Pineapples!

GRIZZLY BEAR

Grizzly Bear started out as Edward's home project. The first songs he wrote were done simply to show his friends, but with the help of Christopher, his buddy who played the drums and helped him record the tracks, these ended up becoming the band's debut album. Soon, multi-instrumentalists Chris and Daniel joined in, which allowed for them to play the album's complex music live. Their third album, *Veckatimest*, earned them international success and appraisal from the critics, with some of its songs being used in television series, movies and ads. Grizzly Bear create truly original melodies with traditional and electronic instruments and vocal harmonies that seem to hypnotise the listener.

BAND MEMBERS
Ed Droste
Daniel Rossen
Christopher Bear
Chris Taylor

FORMED IN 2002

ORIGIN Brooklyn, NY

GENRE Indie Folk, Pop, Psychedelic, Electronic, Experimental

FAMOUS SONGS
Knife
Two Weeks
Yet Again

FLEET FOXES

Seattle boasts more than *Grunge*. Robin and Skyler may have grown in the city that brought us Nirvana and Pearl Jam, but these friends (who were into Bob Dylan, Neil Young and The Beach Boys) preferred *Folk*. They started playing together and in 2006 they recorded their first demo, which caught the interest of Phil Ek, a music producer. Phil quickly realized that Robin was brimming with talent due to his delicate compositions, lyrics and voice. The band members use an incredible number of traditional instruments. In just three years, these flannel-covered, well-tuned foxes became the leading band in this new era of *Folk*.

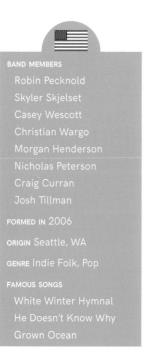

BAND MEMBERS
Robin Pecknold
Skyler Skjelset
Casey Wescott
Christian Wargo
Morgan Henderson
Nicholas Peterson
Craig Curran
Josh Tillman

FORMED IN 2006

ORIGIN Seattle, WA

GENRE Indie Folk, Pop

FAMOUS SONGS
White Winter Hymnal
He Doesn't Know Why
Grown Ocean

MUMFORD & SONS

The band usually plays small and private backstage concerts for their friends after finishing their main concerts.

Marcus started his musical career in London, playing in some *Folk* bands. By that time he'd become acquainted with the members of his future band, united by the shared love of *Folk* music. Despite the band's name, Marcus is not the father of the rest of the line-up; the name was chosen because he's the most visible member and to make it look like it's a family business. The band released their debut album *Sigh No More* in 2009, showcasing their fresh and *Rock*-infused *Folk*. It was a hit, just like the following ones, placing Mumford & Sons squarely on the *Indie Folk* map.

BAND MEMBERS
Marcus Mumford; Winston Marshall; Ben Lovett; Ted Dwane

FORMED IN 2007

ORIGIN London

GENRE Indie Folk, Alternative Rock

FAMOUS SONGS
Little Lion Man; The Cave; I Will Wait

BON IVER

You know how some musicians like to do it all by themselves? Justin is one of them. Legend has it that in 2006 he went to live in an isolated cabin deep in the forest during the winter (in Wisconsin). His heart was broken and his health was shaken. He didn't have much to do apart from watching bears go by and picking up wood for his fireplace, so he started to write songs based on sad and wonderful melodies which result-

he records them alone, when touring he has the help of musicians Sean, Michael and Matthew, among others, so that it works as a band.

BAND MEMBERS
Justin Vernon
Sean Carey
Michael Noyce
Matthew McCaughan

FORMED IN 2006

ORIGIN Eau Claire, WI

GENRE Indie Folk, Pop, Electronic

FAMOUS SONGS
Skinny Love
Calgary
Holocene

ed in a record that became a worldwide hit. This was where the Bon Iver project started and, even though

The name Bon Iver comes from the French expression "bon hiver," which means "good winter."

OTHER MUSICIANS
be all ears

BONNIE 'PRINCE' BILLY
Ohio River Boat Song
I See A Darkness

ELLIOTT SMITH
Waltz #2
Between the Bars

NEUTRAL MILK HOTEL
Two-Headed Boy
Oh Comely

CAT POWER
Metal Heart
Lived in Bars

BADLY DRAWN BOY
Silent Sigh
All Possibilities

ANDREW BIRD
Three White Horses
Tenuousness

SUFJAN STEVENS
Chicago
Flint

SUN KILL MOON
Ben's My Friend
I Love Portugal

DEVENDRA BANHART
I Feel Just Like a Child
Baby

JOANNA NEWSOM
Good Intentions (....)
Baby Birch

BAND OF HORSES
Is There a Ghost
No One's Gonna Love You

FATHER JOHN MISTY
Real Love Baby
Ballad of the Dying Man

WOODS
To Clean
Rain On

ANGEL OLSEN
Windows
Shut Up Kiss Me

You've reached the last section of the book. Here you'll find bands from quite different genres, from MGMT's and Tame Impala's *Neo-psychedelia* to electronic *Pop*, from The XX and African beats-infused *Rock* in Vampire Weekend. All of these musicians love to mix and match styles from previous decades. They also have in common a new way to create music: some recorded their first tracks at home (you can do anything nowadays with a computer!) and, moreover, used the internet to promote their music, as has become standard in this new millennium.

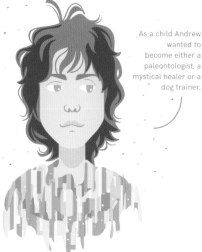

As a child Andrew wanted to become either a paleontologist, a mystical healer or a dog trainer.

Kevin stated that the name of the band came from his childhood memories, leafing through the pages of books on wild animals.

MGMT

Ben and Andrew were freshmen in college when they started to write songs. Originally they called themselves The Management, but since that name had already been taken they changed it to MGMT. Throughout university they started taking music more seriously and in their last year there they started playing live, inviting other musicians to join in. In 2005 they released their first EP, *Time to Pretend*, and the next year their first album, *Oracular Spectacular*. Their songs, filled with keyboards and dance beats, were such a massive hit that even French president Nicolas Sarkozy used their track *Kids* during his campaign. He ended up being sued by the band, as they did not give him permission to use their music. MGMT are still creating great music.

BAND MEMBERS
Andrew VanWyngarden
Ben Goldwasser

FORMED IN 2002

ORIGIN Middletown, CT

GENRE Psychedelic, Pop, Electronic

FAMOUS SONGS
Time to Pretend
Electric Feel
Kids
Flash Delirium

TAME IMPALA

Tame Impala started out as Kevin's individual project. He was a young man fascinated with '60s *Psychedelic Rock*, and recorded tracks at home and shared them on the internet. A label heard his songs and got interested. Kevin sent them a demo with 20 effects-filled songs, and soon after this signed a contract. Even though Kevin sings and plays all of the instruments in the studio, Tame Impala present themselves as a regular band when playing live, with Jay helping out on drums and Dominic on bass. Meanwhile, Cam and Julien came on board. In 2010 they released their debut album, which had some success, but the second one, *Lonerism*, got them lots of compliments and the title of best band to modernize *Psychedelic Rock*.

BAND MEMBERS
Kevin Parker
Jay Watson
Dominic Simper
Julien Barbagallo
Cam Avery

FORMED IN 2007

ORIGIN Perth

GENRE Psychedelic, Pop

FAMOUS SONGS
Elephant
Feels like We Only (...)
The Less I Know (...)

THE XX

Oliver and Romy met each other in kindergarten and created a duo at age 15. They had a wide range of musical tastes, from *R&B* to The Cure and Pixies' *Alternative Rock* to Rihanna's *Pop*. They met the rest of the members of their future band, Jamie and Baria, in high school. After some years playing live, they released their debut album (called simply *The XX*). It creates a dark and melancholic atmosphere that serves as a backdrop to Oliver and Romy's beautiful voices, which can be heard in several duets. By the end of the year Baria left the group and The XX became a trio. The band members don't talk much about their lives; they're quite mysterious.

BAND MEMBERS
Romy Croft
Oliver Sim
Jamie Smith
Baria Qureshi

FORMED IN 2005

ORIGIN London

GENRE Pop, Electronic, Alternative Rock

FAMOUS SONGS
Crystalised
Islands
VCR
Angels
On Hold

Jamie Smith and Romy Croft share a passion for skating.

Ezra used to be an eighth-grade English teacher.

VAMPIRE WEEKEND

Ezra and Chris Tomson were in love with *Punk* and African music, and had a *Rap* project called *L'Homme Run*. Afterwards, they started Vampire Weekend with bass player Chris Baio and guitarist Rostam. They recorded their songs in many unusual places, from college dorms to the family barn. During those initial years, even before releasing their debut album, the band was praised in blogs and websites for their original sound and witty lyrics. The year 2008 saw their self-titled debut album being launched and the long-awaited success arriving: it was considered the 5th best album of the year by *Rolling Stone* magazine. Their energetic *Rock*, inspired by African *Pop* (and by Paul Simon, a singer who had created that mix before) took them on a journey made of great songs and even better lyrics.

BAND MEMBERS
Ezra Koenig
Chris Tomson
Chris Baio
Rostam Batmanglij

FORMED IN 2006

ORIGIN New York, NY

GENRE Alternative Rock, World Music, Pop

FAMOUS SONGS
Mansard Roof
A-Punk
Oxford Comma
Horchata
Cousins

OTHER MUSICIANS
be all ears

ANIMAL COLLECTIVE
The Purple Bottle
Peacebone

DEERHUNTER
Nothing Ever Happened
Helicopter

THE BLACK ANGELS
Entrance Song
Half Believing

BEACH HOUSE
Master of None
Wedding Bell

FOXYGEN
San Francisco
On Blue Mountain

THE WAR ON DRUGS
Under The Pressure
Red Eyes

MOON DUO
Mazes
Sevens

UNKNOWN MORTAL ORCHESTRA
So Good at Being in Trouble
First World Problem

KING GIZZARD AND THE LIZARD WIZARD
Gamma Knife
Billabong Valley

FAT WHITE FAMILY
Touch The Leather
Whitest Boy On The Beach

IDLES
Well Done
Danny Nedelko

NAVIGATE AN ORCHESTRA OF MUSIC GENRES

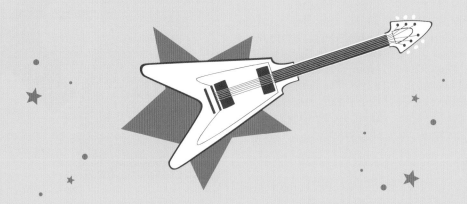

ALTERNATIVE ROCK – Also known as *Indie Rock*. It names some types of *Rock* that are not commercial (that is, made for the masses) but that does not necessarily mean that bands are not sponsored or hired by labels. Not every independent band can be classified as *Alternative Rock* and vice versa. A lot of these bands end up becoming commercial.

ART ROCK – A subgenre of *Rock* that is influenced by *Experimental* music and *Avant-garde*. *Art Rock* favours keyboards instead of guitars. The term *Art Rock* is vague, and can be fused with different genres: *Progressive*, *Punk*, *Folk* or *Experimental*, but always with a tendency towards artistic experimentation.

AVANT-GARDE – A term that defines music that uses innovative techniques, different from what has been traditionally done, trying to be ahead of its time.

BIG BEAT – Electronic music based on fast *Hip-Hop* beats mixed in with *Funk* beats and samples. May include guitar riffs.

BLUES – Appeared at the end of the 19th century out of the African musical tradition in the Southern USA. It is characterized by its sentimental and melancholic tone and slow pace.

BRITPOP – A soft and engaging mixture of *Pop* and *Rock* influenced by '60s British *Pop*, '70s *Glam* and *Punk*, and '80s *Alternative Rock*.

CLASSICAL – Also known as classical art music. It goes back to the 9th century and it is characterized by the complexity of its instrumentation. It can be represented in the form of a symphony, a concerto, an opera, chamber music, etc. Some of its main composers include Vivaldi, Bach, Mozart, Beethoven and Chopin.

COLLEGE ROCK – It's the kind of *Alternative Rock* that used to be played in American colleges and universities for those students who did not enjoy the more mainstream music one could hear on local or national radios.

COUNTRY – Usually made of simple harmonies and a strong beat. It uses stringed instruments (guitar, banjo, etc.) as a melodic base for its ballads and dancing tunes. This style is derived from *Folk* and *Blues*.

DISCO – Dance music genre with pulsating rhythms and repetitive lyrics created for the dance floor. Had its heyday in the mid-70s.

ELECTRONIC – Music that uses sounds originated or transformed by electronic devices, like computers and synthesizers.

EXPERIMENTAL – Genre connected to invention and exploration. Generally speaking, these bands use instruments that are relatively unknown, modified or used in innovative ways, but also sounds that objects make, weird effects and a mixture of quite different genres, like *Electronic* and *Classical*.

FOLK – There are two types of *Folk* music. One is a very old traditional style, of unknown origin. This type of *Folk* (folklore) is characteristic of a people or a culture. In the 1960s a new type of *Folk* was created by Bob Dylan, who mixed traditional music with *Rock and Roll*. That subgenre is known simply as *Folk Rock*.

FOLK PUNK – It combines elements of *Folk* and *Punk*. Gave origin to the subgenre *Celtic Punk* which uses the traditional music from Celtic people, like the Irish, the Scots and the Welsh.

FUNK – Popular North-American music with *Jazz*, *Blues* and *Soul* influences. It is marked by its strong, dance-inducing rhythm.

GARAGE ROCK – Subgenre of *Rock* based on simple electric guitar chords (sometimes with distortion), bass, drums and keyboards. The term *Garage Rock* comes from the notion that bands were often formed by young amateurs rehearsing in the family's garage.

GLAM ROCK – Subgenre of *Rock* that appeared in England by the late '60s. It was characterized by flashy costumes and accessories: glitter, high heels, lipstick, feathers, etc.

GOSPEL – Vocal religious music from the Afro-American community.

GOTHIC ROCK – Subgenre of *Rock* inspired by dark, decadent and melancholic atmospheres. Lyrics are usually personal and introspective and possess a poetic sensibility and a taste for literary romanticism, horror and the supernatural.

GRUNGE – A blend of *Rock*, *Punk* and *Heavy Metal* born in the mid-80s in Seattle. Grunge – meaning dirt or rubbish – describes not only the bands' and fans' visual style (sloppy hair, old and baggy clothes) but also the distorted yet powerful guitar sound.

HARDCORE PUNK – Known as the "second wave" of *Punk*, it has extremely fast beats, short songs, social and political protest lyrics, anger and frustration sung in an aggressive way.

HARD ROCK – It's heavier than conventional *Rock* and is defined by its use of distortion, a strong rhythm section, simple arrangements and a powerful sound based on heavy guitar riffs and complicated solos.

HEAVY METAL – A derivative of *Rock* that's powerful and loud, with fast beats, screaming voices and distorted sounds produced by electric guitars. Lyrics can be hard to understand depending on the way in which they're sung. It gave rise to many subgenres: *Doom Metal*, *Power Metal*, *Speed Metal*, *Thrash Metal*, *Black Metal*, *Death Metal*, and many others.

HIP-HOP – Cultural and musical movement based on four pillars: *Rap*, DJing, Breakdance and Graffiti. *Rap* always has a spoken-rhymes vocal element, while *Hip-Hop* can be purely instrumental. Some of the most famous *Hip-Hop* songs do not contain *Rap*, consisting only of beats, sampling and scratching.

HOUSE – Electronic dance music, usually melodic and featuring vocals. It was influenced by *Disco* music.

INDIE FOLK – A popular genre with *Alternative Rock* musicians that were influenced by *Folk*, combining electric guitar melodies mixed with electronic elements.

INDUSTRIAL – This music genre uses noises, unexpected sounds and anti-melodic structures; it likes to experiment with non-musical elements, synths and distorted guitars, sounds from everyday objects and work tools. Gave origin to the subgenre *Industrial Rock*, which fuses *Rock* and *Industrial* music.

JAZZ – It appeared in the USA at the beginning of the 20th century. It mixes several musical traditions with diverse origins. It is characterized by improvisation. The most commonly used instruments are saxophone, trumpet, piano and double bass.

NEW WAVE – Subgenre of *Rock* born at the same time as *Punk* yet different, as it was based in a combination of *Pop* with *Disco* and *Electronic*. One of its most common characteristics is the use of synthesizers. It gave birth to other subgenres: *Synth-pop* and *New Romantic*.

NO WAVE – Appeared as a reaction (and a pun) to *New Wave*. It was an artistic and musical movement defined by experimentation and performative art. These musicians preferred to experiment with noises and dissonance and based their music on *Jazz* and *Funk*.

NOISE ROCK – Subgenre that mixes *Rock* with noise, constructing songs with conventional instruments but with a lot of distortion and electronic effects.

NU METAL – Mixes elements of *Metal* with other genres, like *Hip-Hop*, *Alternative Rock*, *Funk*, *Grunge* and *Industrial*. One of its main characteristics is to combine aggressive riffs with *Pop* structures and screams with melodic voices.

POP – Music born out of the UK and the US, characterized by simple melodies, repetitive rhythm and strong beats. It is generally seen as a synonym for "popular music," that is, music for general audiences.

POST-PUNK – It started in England after *Punk*'s heyday. The genre has its roots in the *Punk* movement, yet it's more introspective, complex and melancholic.

PROGRESSIVE ROCK – It appeared in England in the second half of the '60s, mixing *Pop* and *Rock* with other genres of a more complex harmony, like *Classical* music and *Jazz*. Throughout the years many subgenres appeared, like *Symphonic Rock*, *Space Rock*, *Krautrock*, *Progressive Metal* and *Symphonic Metal*.

PSYCHEDELIC – Subgenre of *Rock* associated to the hippie culture. Its main characteristics include guitars, special sound effects and hypnotic atmospheres, many times adding contrasting and experimental harmonies.

PUNK – Music genre characterized by fast and noisy tracks, where songs usually cover anarchist and revolutionary political ideas.

RAP – Music genre in which rhymes are spoken in a fast and rhythmical way. It can be performed a capella (without other instruments) or with a musical backdrop called beatbox. *Rap* singers are known as rappers or MCs (short for Master of Ceremonies). It gave rise to numerous subgenres like *Rap Rock*, *Rap Metal*, *Gangsta Rap* and others.

R&B – Short for *Rhythm and Blues*, it combines *Blues*, *Gospel* and *Soul*. These days it is associated to artists like Alicia Keys, Beyoncé and Rihanna, who mix it up with *Pop* and *Hip-Hop*.

REGGAE – Jamaican music genre born in the 1960s, characterized by the usage of simple melodies and syncopated and repetitive rhythms.

ROCKABILLY – One of the first *Rock and Roll* subgenres. Its name combines the words *Rock* and *Hillbilly*, being the latter a reference to *Country* music, which used to be called *Hillbilly* music in the '40s and '50s.

ROCK AND ROLL – Popular music characterized by strong beats and rhythms, usually played by groups of musicians (usually vocalists, guitarists, bass players and drummers) using electrically amplified instruments. It is frequently connected to a young and rebellious spirit.

SHOCK ROCK – It's not exactly a genre; it's a term for artists who combine *Rock* music or *Heavy Metal* music with theatrical live performances highlighting shock value. Performances may include violent or provocative behavior from the artists, costumes, masks, or face paint, or special effects such as pyrotechnics or fake blood. *Shock Rock* includes elements of horror.

SKA – It was born in Jamaica in the late 1950s. It combines Caribbean elements like *Mento* and *Calypso* and North-American ones like *Jazz* and *Rhythm and Blues*.

SOUL – Popular North-American music influenced by *Jazz*, *Gospel* and *Blues*. It has well-defined rhythms and very expressive and emotional voices.

SURF ROCK – Subgenre of *Rock* associated with *surf* culture. It gave rise to two formats: instrumental *Surf Rock*, based on electric guitar and no voices, and vocal *Surf Pop*, made of ballads or rhythmic songs with strong harmonies.

TECHNO – Electronic dance music with strong beats and no vocals. It favours futuristic themes and sounds to make it look as if it's coming from the future.

TRIP HOP – A combination of *Hip-Hop* and slow *Electronic*, marked by slower beats and by the usage of conventional instruments, seductive voices and hypnotic atmospheres. It usually includes samples.

WORLD MUSIC – Also known as Ethnic music, it refers to the traditional music of a given culture or people, regardless of its origin.

GLOSSARY

A CAPPELLA – Vocal music without instrumental accompaniment.

ALBUM – Multi-track musical piece recorded in a particular format. It can have various formats: vinyl, cassette, CD, pen drive, etc.

AMPLIFIER – Device that can increase the sound of instruments. It is vital for electric instruments.

ARTISTIC MOVEMENT – A collective of artists who create pieces that share common ideas in a given place, for a restricted time period.

BEATBOXING – Percussion sound reproduction performed with voice, mouth and nose. It also involves vocal mimicking of other musical instruments and sound effects.

BILLBOARD – Weekly North-American magazine specialized in the music industry. It includes charts where songs and albums are ordered according to the amount of copies sold.

BRAILLE – Tactile writing system used by people who are fully or partially visually impaired.

CBGB – New York club known as the birthplace of several renowned bands, mainly connected to *Punk*.

CD (COMPACT DISC) – Popular music recording medium.

CHORD – Simultaneous production of three or more musical notes.

CULT BAND – Band that has a small yet very faithful number of fans.

DEMO – Recording that contains a sample of the main musical ideas from a band or a musician.

DISC JOCKEY (DJ) – Artist that selects and plays music, be it previously recorded or produced on the fly for a given target audience: radio, dance floor, clubs, etc.

DRUM MACHINE – Electronic device that produces percussion sounds.

EP (EXTENDED PLAY) – Vinyl or CD recording that is longer than a single yet shorter than an album.

FAN – Person who really likes a band or an artist.

FEEDBACK – Continuous, piercing sound that is produced when a microphone or a guitar pickup captures, through the speakers, the same sound it is reproducing.

GOLDEN GLOBES – Cinema and television awards given out by the Hollywood Foreign Press Association.

GRAMMY – Music industry awards presented by The Recording Academy.

GROUPIE – A fan who tries constantly to be with or near the band or artist.

GUINNESS RECORD – A registry of a feat in which the holder is the best in the world in the specific category being registered.

HIT – Something that presents good results, good sales or lots of popularity.

IMPROVISATION – Music created or executed without prior preparation.

JUG BAND – A band that uses primitive or improvised instruments (such as jugs, washboards, and kazoos) to play *Blues*, *Jazz* and *Folk* music.

JUKEBOX – Machine that contains a great variety of recorded songs that can be reproduced by selection of track and insertion of a coin in a slot.

KAZOO – Instrument that adds a kind of buzzing to the human voice.

LABEL – Company that invests in the recording and promotion of artists and that produces songs and albums.

LO-FI – Short for low fidelity: music recorded with less quality than the standard at the time. It also refers to a music genre.

MANAGER – A representative of a band or a musician with other members of the music industry like labels, clubs, etc.

MCS – Short for Master of Ceremonies. The MC is the host who presents the DJ or a rapper that sings their own material.

MUSIC CHARTS – List of songs or albums ordered by their sales figures.

MUSIC GENRE – Categories that share common elements. Genres define and classify artists and their music.

MUSIC LOVER – One who feels passion and enthusiasm for music.

MUSIC VIDEO – Short film created specifically to accompany a song.

NOBEL – Awards given out by several Swedish and Norwegian institutions that recognize outstanding people in scientific, artistic and social areas.

OSCAR – Cinema awards given out by the Academy of Motion Picture Arts and Sciences in Los Angeles, USA.

PICKUP – Electrical component that converts guitar or bass strings' vibrations into an electrical current sent to an amplifier and heard as sound through a speaker.

PRODUCER – Person who coaches and guides the musicians and is responsible for finishing up a recording to get it ready for release.

PULITZER – Awards for achievements in journalism, literature and musical composition attributed by the University of Columbia, USA.

RECORD – Circular medium (usually vinyl) on which songs are recorded.

RIFF – Progression of chords, intervals or musical notes that are repeated in the context of a song.

ROADIE – A technician who helps the bands in concert.

SAMPLE – A piece of a song that is used directly in another song.

SAMPLING – Usage of a sample as an instrument or sound in a song.

SCRATCHING – Musical technique used by a DJ to produce sounds by "scratching" the vinyl record back and forth repeatedly.

SILVER, GOLD AND PLATINUM RECORDS – Prizes given to records sold in great quantity. Exact figures vary depending on the country.

SINGLE – Recording medium that only contains one or two songs, usually used for promotion of an album.

SOLO (INSTRUMENTAL) – Part of a song played or sung by one artist only.

SOLOIST (ARTIST) – An artist who is the sole author of a given work.

STAR – Artist who has reached a very high level of recognition and success.

STYLE – Personal way of expressing oneself, be it in the way one talks, writes, composes, sings, dresses, etc. It also identifies and characterizes a given group or artistic movement.

SYNTHESIZER (SYNTH) – Music instrument that generates electrical signals that are converted into sounds by amplifiers, speakers or headphones.

TOP – The highest section of a music chart.

TOUR – A programmed list of destinations where bands or artists play concerts.

VOCODER – Instrument that synthesizes the human voice.

ACKNOWLEDGMENTS

To Nuno, without whom this project would not have been possible.
To Leonardo, for his support and collaboration.
To my brother Nuno Nabais and my friend Tiago Almeida for those initial and most
important musical influences.

TO THE FRIENDS WHO SENT THEIR TOP ARTISTS LISTS:

Aristides Duarte
Carlos "Kaló" Mendes (Tédio Boys/ Wraygunn/
   Bunny Ranch/ The Twist Connection)
César Augusto Vasco
Eduardo Morais
Fernando Ribeiro (Moonspell)
Gaspar Garção
Hugo Amado
Hugo Trindade (Sea Groove & The Ocean Travellers/
   Hugo Trindade Trio)
Isidro Lisboa
João Silva "Jorri" (a Jigsaw)
José Alberto Vasco
José Miguel "Toni Lee Pierce Osterberg"
Luís Rainho
Luís "Van" Seixas (Sci-Fi Industries)

Miguel Ângelo (Delfins)
Miguel Ribeiro (The Gift)
Nuno Lorvão
Nuno Nabais
Ondina Pires (Pop Dell'Arte/ The Great Lesbian Show)
Paula Guerra
Paulo Alexandre
Paulo Louro
Pedro Silva
Ricardo Baldo
Samuel Jerónimo
Valério Romão
Vasco Sousa
Victor Torpedo (The Parkinsons)
Vitorino Coragem

TO MY MUSIC TEMPLES:

Bar Ben
Incógnito
Clinic

THE BOOK ENDS HERE
BUT THE MUSIC LIVES ON.
EVERY DAY, NEW GROUPS OF FRIENDS
GET TOGETHER IN THEIR GARAGES,
UNITED BY THE ROCK THEY LISTEN TO
AND THAT THEY PLAY IN THEIR INSTRUMENTS.

WHO KNOWS...
THE NEXT BAND THAT ENTERS THE HISTORY OF ROCK MIGHT BE YOURS!

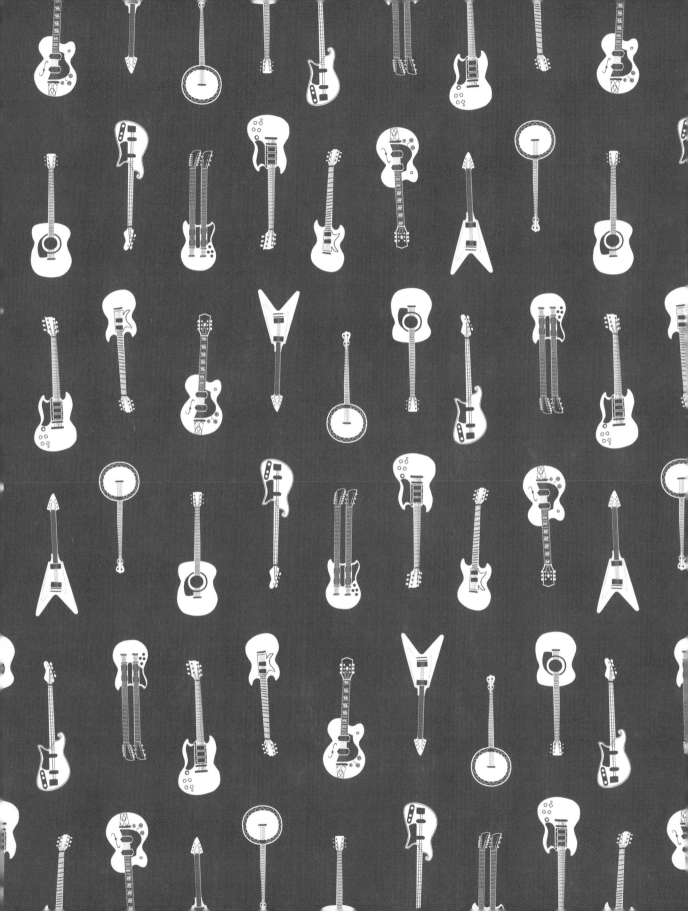